THE MYTH OF INDEPENDENCE

The Myth of Independence

ZULFIKAR ALI BHUTTO

London
OXFORD UNIVERSITY PRESS
LAHORE   KARACHI   DACCA
1969

Oxford University Press, Ely House, London W.1

GLASGOW   NEW YORK   TORONTO   MELBOURNE   WELLINGTON
CAPE TOWN   SALISBURY   IBADAN   NAIROBI   LUSAKA   ADDIS ABABA
BOMBAY   CALCUTTA   MADRAS   KARACHI   LAHORE   DACCA
KUALA LUMPUR   HONG KONG   TOKYO   SINGAPORE

Printed in Great Britain by
Butler & Tanner Ltd, Frome and London

Dedicated to
The Sovereign People of Pakistan

Acknowledgements

In expressing my appreciation to Mr. J. A. Rahim for taking the trouble to read the manuscript, and for making valuable suggestions, I am not in any way absolving myself from the sole responsibility for what is written in this book.

Acknowledgements are also due to the following: to Hamish Hamilton and Harper & Row for permission to quote from *The Strategy of Peace* by John F. Kennedy; to Jonathan Cape Ltd. and Curtis Brown Ltd. for permission to quote from *Verdict on India* by Beverley Nichols; and to Chatto & Windus Ltd. and Oxford University Press, Inc., for permission to quote from *The Continent of Circe* by N. C. Chaudhuri.

Preface

When in 1958 I entered upon my career in high public office at the comparatively early age of thirty, as Minister for Commerce in the Martial Law Government, the situation Pakistan found itself in was such that every decision of any importance, even as regards matters that ought to have been of purely internal concern, was affected by some aspect, real or imaginary, of international relations, especially of commitments to the United States of America. For me there was no escape from problems of international relations, whether I was in charge of the Ministries of Commerce and later of Fuel, Power and Natural Resources, or Minister for Industries, a portfolio which I held during 1962–3.

The study of history, an acquaintance with the problems of underdeveloped countries, and my own penchant for international politics justified, I imagined, my ambition to serve Pakistan as its Foreign Minister. That ambition was fulfilled when I was made Foreign Minister in January 1963, on the death of Mr. Mohammad Ali of Bogra.

Before that date, however, I had had to deal with international problems of fundamental importance to the interests of Pakistan. In December 1960, in my capacity as Minister for Fuel, Power and Natural Resources, I went to Moscow to conduct negotiations with the Soviet Union for an oil agreement. I mention this fact because it marked the point at which our relations with the Soviet Union, most unsatisfactory until then, began to improve.

On my return from the famous General Assembly Session of 1960 which was attended by Premier Khrushchev, Presidents Nasser and Soekarno, Mr. Macmillan, Pandit Nehru, Señor Fidel Castro, and many other eminent statesmen, I was convinced that the time had arrived for the Government of Pakistan to review and revise its foreign policy. I accordingly offered suggestions to my Government, all of which were finally accepted. This was before I became Foreign Minister. The ground was thus prepared for my work, by changes introduced at my own insistence, when I took charge officially of the conduct of foreign policy as Foreign Minister.

The reader will discover for himself in the pages of this book what opinions I hold, what my attitude is to world problems, what mistakes I believe were committed by Pakistan in dealing with foreign powers—particularly with Global Powers—and how those mistakes may be remedied; what my proposals are for a foreign policy adequate to avert the dangers which now threaten the country. It would be pointless to attempt to summarize these views within the brief compass of a Preface. Nevertheless, it is worth emphasizing that the policy of close relations with China, which I formulated and put into operation, is indispensable to Pakistan; that in dealing with Great Powers one must resist their pressures by all possible means available, when they offend against the Nation's welfare; and that compromises leading to the settlement of disputes by default or in an inequitable manner strike at the roots of national security, even existence. If I assume responsibility for certain policies, I also admit that I made every effort to carry them into effect until I left office in June 1966.

Though tempted to write at greater length about the Indo-Pakistan war of 1966 and the subsequent Tashkent Declaration, I decided, for various reasons, to defer discussion of these and other topics to a later date. The truth of this chapter of history has yet to be told.

I confess that this book has been written in haste, in circumstances over which I had no control, in a race against time which is dragging Pakistan, with giant strides, to the crossroads whence all ways but one lead to destruction.

Z. A. B.

Karachi,
November 1967

Contents

Plates

CHAPTER 1

The Struggle for Equality

On 19 May 1954, after some hard negotiations, Pakistan and the United States of America concluded the Mutual Defence Assistance Agreement and entered upon a period of association euphemistically called a 'special relationship'. For over twelve years, the United States provided Pakistan with considerable economic and military assistance. In 1959, misunderstandings arose in the relations between the two countries and have since grown and multiplied, especially after the Sino-Indian conflict. Relations have followed a chequered course, sometimes bearing on economic matters and sometimes, more profoundly, on political issues. The pendulum has swung from one extreme to the other, from association to estrangement. There was a time when Pakistan was described as the most 'allied ally' of the United States and, to the chagrin of other 'client States' of Asia, it was asserted by President Ayub Khan, in an address to the United States' Congress in 1961, that Pakistan was the only country in the continent where the United States Armed Forces could land at any moment for the defence of the 'free world'. When, during the U-2 episode, in an attempt at refined diplomacy, the United States prevaricated with ambiguous statements, Pakistan, more royalist than the monarch, openly admitted that the aircraft had taken off from Pakistan and that, as a staunch ally of the United States, Pakistan was within its rights to allow it to do so.

In less than a quarter of a century, Pakistan's relations with the United States and India have completed a cycle in each case. Vigorous efforts have been made to drag Pakistan away from the posture of confrontation to co-operation with India and, in this very process, relations with the United States have changed dramatically from those of the most 'allied ally' to the point at which it is alleged that there is 'collusion' between Pakistan and the United States' principal antagonist—the

People's Republic of China. How these twin cycles have been completed offers an exciting study of the interplay of a host of related factors: national ethos, geography, a turbulent past, and hoary traditions. The pride and passions of an ancient people stirred by nascent Asian nationalism are involved. The story ranges over a wide horizon: from religion to economics, from geography to politics, from history to myth, from race to genocide. In this web the United States has been entangled at almost every point. This book attempts to examine one facet of this many-sided situation.

Although, in the recent past, relations between Pakistan and the United States have been characterized by a series of vicissitudes, only the United States' decision to terminate military assistance to Pakistan—a country to which it is technically still bound by the obligations of a Mutual Defence Treaty and an association in the defence alliances of CENTO and SEATO— finally put a stop to the special relationship. On Wednesday 12 April 1967 a State Department spokesman announced in Washington:

We have concluded an extensive review of our policy with regard to the provision of military equipment to India and Pakistan and have decided that we will not resume grant of military assistance which has been suspended since September, 1965. We are therefore closing the U.S. Military Assistance Advisory Group (MAAG) in Pakistan and the U.S. Military Supply Mission in India (USMSMI). This process is expected to be completed by July 1, 1967, in both cases.

We have also decided to remove present U.S. Government restrictions on the kinds of spare parts, which may be sold to India and Pakistan for previously supplied equipment. Henceforth we will be prepared to consider, on a case-by-case basis, all requests for export permits covering the cash purchase of spare parts.

The United States will continue to keep its military sales policy under careful review to ensure that it is not contributing to an arms race between India and Pakistan. We strongly hope that both countries will make progress in resolving the problems and differences that divide them and that they accord an increasing priority in the allocation of their resources to agricultural and industrial development.[1]

---

[1] *Dawn* (Karachi), 13 April 1967.

This decision was of far-reaching consequence to the future of the sub-continent and of Asia as a whole, which is now replacing Europe as the principal source of crises affecting the gravest issues of war and peace. For centuries Europe was the centre from which conflicts radiated. This is not to say that Asia was free from trouble while Europe remained in the grip of revolutions and upheavals. History has not, so far, blessed any part of mankind with absolute tranquillity. What has happened is that the eye of the hurricane has shifted to Asia, where a cruel war is being fought in Vietnam, on the outcome of which hinges the fate of people everywhere. That ravaged country is engaged in a life-and-death struggle, for the moment confined to Vietnam; but it is quite possible that, when it reaches a certain critical point, the war will pass its present frontiers, turning the land mass of Asia into an immense battle-field and, perhaps, spreading its consuming flames beyond.

How close the world could come to the brink of a total conflagration was seen at the time of the recent war in the Middle East. The crisis preceding that war threatened to undo the *détente* between the Soviet Union and the United States. That this did not happen and the Soviet Union stepped back should not mislead us into thinking that the Soviet Union will always step back, so jeopardizing its claim to world leadership. The fighting between the Arab states and Israel put west Asia and south-east Asia together in the same furnace of war, making people fear that their joint sparks might set fire to the whole world. In both the origin and termination of this five-day war there was a direct connection traceable to Vietnam. But for the United States' deep involvement in Vietnam and the Soviet Union's increasing concern with that war, the crisis in the Middle East would neither have erupted so suddenly nor ended so abruptly. Thus no major political event, particularly in Asia, can be divorced from the Vietnam war with regard both to origin and result.

The one-dimensional approach to diplomacy is wrong. Although it is a natural propensity of people to think in terms of their own situation, the global situation defies this limited approach. World developments have now become so complex and interconnected that no important decision tolls the bell for one people alone. The panoply of politics is no longer parochial in nature. The actions of all nations, and particularly of the Great Powers, are influenced by a multitude of considerations covering a vast field.

Significant decisions which seem to affect Pakistan only have, in reality, a wider relevance. The escalation of the war in Vietnam would become a simple matter if it concerned Vietnam and the United States alone, but every step in the escalation has to be measured in terms of responses not only of Vietnam and the United States but also of China and the Soviet Union among other states. America's decision to terminate military assistance to Pakistan has to be considered in the wider perspective of its Asian implications. The stakes are very much higher than they appear to be, and this has to be recognized in the protection of larger national interests.

If international events are looked at from one angle only, the United States' decision to terminate military assistance to Pakistan would seem to be an abrupt and arbitrary act. If, however, world issues are objectively analysed, not in the context of bilateral relations but globally, the decision appears to be neither abrupt nor arbitrary. It is essential to examine both this important decision and the future course of American–Pakistani relations in a comprehensive and objective manner in order to determine how we stand now and how we may yet stand with the other nations of the world. Attempts to foresee the future can help the formulation of accurate political judgements and the enlightenment of our people as to the kind of problems or hazards that might have to be faced in a world which moves uncertainly between co-existence and co-annihilation.

Ever since man left his caves to seek and fashion more favourable conditions of life, he has been in conflict with his fellows; all have been moved by the same impulses and all have striven towards the same or similar ends. With the growth of civilization the struggle for existence has found its highest expression in relations between states. Aristotle observed that: 'It is evident that the state is a creation of nature, and that man is by nature a political animal. And he who by nature and not by mere accident is without a state is either above humanity or below it.' Behind the development of culture and science lies the human urge, expressed by means of the state, to improve the conditions of life within the collective unit. The conflicts that arise between groups, each seeking its own interest, are the ingredients of history. The organized group in its highest form, the nation-state, is the most predatory, as it is the most exacting towards the individuals that compose it. The conflicts within such groups and the conflicts between them create a form of protest, which is the struggle for equality. This began with the dawn of civilization. Records remain of the early cradles of conflict in the Tigris–Euphrates valley and in the Indus valley civilization about 4000 years before the birth of Christ. The civilizations that followed—Egypt, Babylon, Greece, Carthage and Rome—all have known the same struggle. Ancient Persia and Byzantium, the Empire of the Ottomans, the colonial outposts of the British and the French Empires, and Nazi Germany have all played their role in the same drama—greed urging domination and colliding with the struggle for equality. Whenever, in this drive for domination, the flames were momentarily extinguished and the sword replaced in its sheath, the struggle still continued under different names and in different forms. Domination has been justified as the survival of the fittest; it has been given the name of the White Man's Burden; it has been glorified by theories of the exclusive responsibilities of the Master Race. Today that ancient struggle is epitomized in the creed of democracy against dictatorship.

Oppressed people everywhere, bound by the chains of colonialism, were urged, not so long ago, to participate in the struggle against Nazism in order to free humanity from tyranny. Immediately after the defeat of Nazism, many nations in Asia gained their political independence. After nearly two centuries of enslavement, India and Pakistan were among the principal states in our Asian continent to become free in that sense. Twenty years of independence have revealed to the people of Pakistan and India the sharp difference that really exists between independence and sovereign equality. The struggle to attain sovereign equality continues undiminished. Foreign domination has been replaced by foreign intervention, and the power to make decisions radically affecting the lives of our peoples has been curtailed by the cannons of neo-colonialism. The war against Nazism has been followed by the cold war between the United States and the Soviet Union, which was further intensified by the end of Mao Tse-Tung's long march to victory in 1949.

Since Independence, Pakistan's foreign relations have evolved in stages; partly influenced by changing conditions and partly by sentiment and subjective judgements which invariably influence the thoughts of new nations. To arrive at a true and unbiased appreciation of Pakistan's role in the sub-continent, in Asia and in the world, it is necessary to examine relations with states not on an *ad hoc* basis, but on that of a deeper consideration of world events and the objective facts that influence relations of nation-states, large and small. Political theorists, particularly in Pakistan, are inclined to make policy assessments out of immediate developments and jump to hasty and arbitrary conclusions. Difficulties arise from our habit of reaching rigid conclusions and persisting in them. It is necessary to make a departure from old habits of thought for the sake of a clearer appreciation of facts. Indeed, the true implications of recent happenings can only be judged if every major development is viewed in its proper place in the vast jig-saw puzzle of international power politics. My narrative must therefore begin at the beginning—the Partition of the sub-continent shortly after the defeat of Hitler's Third Reich.

CHAPTER 2

Global Powers and Small Nations

Since the end of the Second World War, a new political situation has developed which, perhaps because it is so evident, is not always seen in its correct perspective and its implications sufficiently understood. Up to 1939 it could be said that the Great Powers were:

1. The United States of America
2. The United Kingdom
3. France
4. Germany
5. The Soviet Union
6. Japan
7. Italy

The traditional method of conducting foreign affairs in the nineteenth and the first half of the twentieth centuries was by means of regional alliances formed to maintain a balance of power among the grouping of the Great Powers with the assistance of the smaller nations. Peace was preserved by maintaining this very delicate balance, and peace was disturbed only when the balance, at any given time, tilted in favour of one group or the other. In those days, the smaller nations could influence the policy and the alignment of Great Powers by indulging in various political permutations and combinations.

All this has changed today with the emergence of Global Powers which, in addition to having all the attributes of Great Powers in the classical sense, are at the same time much more powerful and play a larger role in determining the destinies of people all over the world. The emergence of these Powers in the last twenty years has changed the whole concept of conducting affairs of state. The task of smaller nations, in which category all the developing nations fall, in determining their relationship with Global Powers and in furthering their

B

national interests has become more complex and difficult. The small nation which does not understand the new rules of diplomacy is doomed to frustration, a sense of helplessness, isolation and, perhaps, eventual extinction. As a developing nation, Pakistan must understand how to conduct its affairs in this new situation.

What is a Great Power today and what was a Great Power only a few decades ago is a distinction worth examining. In the imperial age the area of influence and control of a Great Power was regional rather than global. Alexander the Great sought to conquer the world, but his world was a small one. The Roman legions swept across Europe and parts of Asia and Africa, but there was more to the world than the lands where the mandate of Rome prevailed. Charlemagne held sway over Europe, but the political Europe of his day did not extend very far east. Ghengiz Khan's hordes galloped across Asia and parts of Europe, but their conquests were of no lasting consequence to the world at large. Napoleon dreamt of a world order that met its doom in the ashes of Moscow. Hitler was moved by a similar ambition, but he too was driven back from the gates of Moscow.

From Alexander to Hitler, many a conqueror set out to subjugate the world but failed. Enormous territories in more than one continent did come under the yoke of one imperial Power or another, but not for long. The sun did not set on the vast British Empire, but even at the height of their power the British had to contend with the ambitions of other imperial Powers—notably, those of Spain, France, and Germany—so that the world neither fell under the hegemony of any one imperial Power, nor was divided by a pact between two Super-Powers. At the end of the Second World War, when the Axis Powers were shattered, the Allied armies had the world at their command; but, even before hostilities had ended, the conflict of interests between Allied Powers and Soviet Russia became apparent. The authority of the old imperialist Powers like Britain, France, and the Netherlands had diminished to such an extent that they were soon forced to relinquish their overseas empires. Into this void stepped the only two Powers which had emerged strong and victorious out of the Second World War—the United States and the Soviet Union. Inexorably filling the political vacuum, they pushed forward their areas of influence both in the east and in the west. In the west, they reached and confronted each other in Berlin and central Europe. In the east, the Soviets extended their influence to the Pacific; while the United States moved into Japan and the Philippines, and temporarily bolstered up the dying French Empire in south-east Asia. Since, traditionally, the United States had not been an imperialist Power in the sense of physically occupying foreign territories—except for the Philippines and some dependencies in the Caribbean—and since the Soviet Union, by reason of its doctrine of Marxism, also could not justify physical possession of foreign territory, a new type of struggle emerged. This was the beginning of neo-colonialism. It no longer became necessary to control the destinies of smaller countries by any jurisdiction over their territories.

The main purpose of imperialism was to exploit the resources of the colonies. Vast territories were divided and distributed among the imperial Powers, which then drained the resources of the subject peoples. With the end of imperialism in its classical form, only the system of exploitation underwent a transformation. As the colonial Powers withdrew from their colonies, the policy of 'divide and rule' became obsolete and was replaced by that of 'unite and rule' to meet the challenge of new times, although to achieve the same objective. The changed conditions necessitated a change in the method. In the past the colonies were exploited separately by each imperial Power. Now that these Powers have vacated their possessions, it has become necessary for them to merge the resources of the former colonies into groupings for better collective exploitation. As the position of the exploiters has changed, so also it has become necessary to change that of the exploited. Previously the imperial Powers went separately about their missions of exploitation. Now that they have joined together for their common advantage, it becomes equally necessary for them that their former colonies should pool their resources to facilitate exploitation. The new situation calls for corresponding adjustments both in the former colonies and in the former colonizing countries to make market conditions more suitable for exploitation. Larger markets generate greater exports and imports on terms favourable to the advanced nations of the West. They encourage increased consumption of goods and a more systematic exploitation of resources. They facilitate the manipulation of prices internationally. There are many advantages, most of them accruing to the former colonial Powers. The security interests of the 'free world' are better served, but economic exploitation remains the principal concern. This is the inevitable adjustment in the transition from colonialism to neo-colonialism, which is why our independence remains a myth.

The West, which in the past showed little sympathy for the struggle of subjugated people to unite, has suddenly found the unity of former colonial peoples to be desirable; so much so that in many places it is being imposed on erstwhile colonies. Everywhere 'co-operation' has become a key word. We are not opposed to unity: indeed, we want the unity of Afro-Asian countries, but a unity voluntarily achieved, on terms of equality, and without foreign interference. Unity must be achieved for the benefit of the people concerned and not for the benefit of foreign Powers and their agents. It should be put in the service of the people and not at the command of foreign forces. Our people must have the freedom to make their own decisions in favour of unity. This kind of unity is opposed by foreign interests, which seek to impose unity for purposes of exploitation in the economic and military fields. There is a fundamental difference between unity willingly forged by a people and that forcibly imposed, which is only a continuation of the Roman peace. Unity which seeks to end exploitation is invariably resisted by foreign Powers determined to retain their privileges in one form or another or fearful of losing them. It goes without saying that the West does not want the unity of, or co-operation between, states that want to assert their independence and control their resources in their own interests. In such cases every effort is made to divide and weaken them. Indeed, in Vietnam the United States is bleeding itself white to prevent the unity of the North and the South. The same applies to Korea. Sometimes circumstances may conspire to make it expedient to support the division of non-Communist states, as was reluctantly done in the sub-continent and not so reluctantly done in the Middle East. These are, however, exceptional cases; such divisions being tolerated or supported, as the case may be, to prevent greater catastrophes or to comply with exceptional interests. The formula of 'unite and rule' obviously cannot be applied everywhere, but as a general proposition it is irre-futable. Most commonly it is applied to the pliable under-developed nations, especially 'committed' states with leaders who make their countries readily susceptible to economic and military exploitation. In the selection of the pliable states it must be remembered that the classification of aligned and non-aligned nations is no longer a yard-stick. It has become obsolete. Indonesia and Ghana are non-aligned, but both are now com-mitted to the West. The changing realities have made the classification more flexible, but essentially only the pliable states, whether aligned or non-aligned, fall within the category of those whose unity is desirable. The Western Powers seek to impose unity where it serves their purposes; unless division will serve them better, as in the case of Syria and Egypt. The efforts to keep the Indo-Pakistan sub-continent united and the sub-sequent manœuvres to create federations in Asia, Africa, and the Middle East have to be interpreted in this neo-colonial context. Since the end of the Second World War the West has tried to create artificial federations in former colonies, even to the extent of bringing together under one order princes divided by centuries of feud. This was attempted in India and achieved in Malaysia and more recently in the Persian Gulf.

The end of imperialism and the emergence of Global Powers have changed the whole concept of a Great Power. Its interests are now fundamentally global and its instrument of expansion is ideology instead of the gunboat. The aim of a Great Power is no longer to subjugate the world in the conventional sense, but to control the minds of men and gain the allegiance of the leaders of underdeveloped nations, through economic domina-tion and other devices, without necessarily interfering directly. In the age of neo-colonialism the physical occupation of terri-tories by a Global Power is not necessary, as the objectives of its global policy can be achieved by indirect exploitation and various kinds of inducement. The multitude of powerful but invisible devices and agencies operating more or less through remote control now bring the same result that physical sub-jugation used to in the past. Modern means of communications make it possible for Great Powers to dictate and direct the daily lives of people all over the world without having to exercise a day-to-day overt control. In this modern lust for ideological and neo-colonial supremacy, the Great Powers have entered into an alarming global rivalry in every corner of the world.

What factors make a Global Power? It is not the extent of territory alone nor the material resources and economic wealth; it is not only a question of scientific and technological excellence; it is not only a matter of ideology; it is in fact, a combination of all these elements. India and Brazil are large in territory, but neither is a Global Power. Czechoslovakia and Belgium might be able to develop sophisticated weapons, but neither can aspire to be a Global Power. The Great Powers of yesterday, such as France and Britain, are now only marginal Global Powers. Now and for as long as it can reasonably be predicted there will be only three genuine Global Powers: the United States of America, the Soviet Union, and the People's Republic of China. Europe as a continent is capable of becoming a fourth Global Power, but this would need an accommodation between Eastern and Western Europe and, among other conditions, the political and institutional collaboration between France, Germany, and Britain. The emergence of a 'European Europe' as a Global Power would help to stabilize peace and is desirable, but it does not appear to be an immediate possibility.

The question before the smaller nations of today is how they should conduct their affairs in such a manner as to safeguard their basic interests; to retain their territorial integrity and to continue to exercise independence in their relationship with the Global Powers as well as with the smaller nations. The relationship between the Global Powers and the smaller countries is on an unequal footing, whereby the former can exact a multitude of concessions without responding in sufficient, let alone equal, measure. No small nation can possibly bring a Global Power under its influence on the plea of justice or because of the righteousness of its cause. In the ultimate analysis, it is not the virtue of the cause that becomes the determining factor, but the cold self-interest of the Global Powers which shapes their policy, and this self-interest has better chances of prevailing in an endless and unequal confrontation between a Global Power and smaller nations.

Should the smaller nations therefore obediently follow the dictates of Global Powers and exchange their independence for material gains and promises of economic prosperity? The answer is an emphatic 'No'. Caught in the nutcracker of the global conflict the underdeveloped nations might in despair conclude that they can only marginally influence the *status quo*, that in reality they have no independent choice but to trim their policies to the requirements of one Global Power or another. This is an unnecessarily pessimistic view, a negation of the struggle of man, expressed through the nation-state, to be free. The force of freedom must triumph because it is stronger than any other force for which man will lay down his life. It is still possible for the smaller nations, with adroit handling of their affairs, to maintain their independence and retain flexibility of action in their relationship with Global Powers.

It would be inexpedient, and perhaps dangerous, for smaller nations to identify themselves completely with the total interests of one Global Power to the exclusion of the others. Common interest and the pattern of events may make it necessary for a small nation to be more closely associated with one Global Power than with another, but, even so, it is not impossible for it to maintain normal relations with the others on the basis of honourable bilateral relations. When the national interests of a state clash with the interests of a Global Power, it would be preferable to isolate the area of conflict in the direct dealings with that Great Power. A workable equilibrium should be sought independent of the point on which vital interests differ, provided, of course, that the segregation of conflicting interests is not only possible but is scrupulously reciprocal. Every reasonable effort should be made to put into action preventive diplomacy to avoid Global Power interventions which subject the weaker nations to suffer from punitive diplomacy. If this, however, is not found to be feasible, it is better to make the position clear by taking a stand against encroachment. It is preferable to have one sharp crisis and a firm position than to permit procrastination to create conditions of permanent crisis. In such a situation, every subsequent crisis will do greater harm to the smaller Power until eventually the Global Power overwhelms it. So, if insulation is not possible, it is better to take a positive position and evolve a new pattern of understanding.

Pressure is both a worm and a monster. It is a worm if you stamp on it, but it becomes a monster if you recoil. In 1962

Burma took a firm line with the United States when it considered it had no honourable alternative course. For a brief
period there were strains in its relations with the United States,
but now relations are better. Both states had to find a new
relationship the moment it was understood that inroads would
not be tolerated. Cambodia, similarly, has demonstrated commendable firmness in dealing with the global interests of the
United States. More recently both Burma and Cambodia have
taken a firm line with China as well. Indeed, during the height
of the cultural revolution, the latter threatened to withdraw its
ambassador from Peking. Had it not been for the intervention
of Chou En-Lai, this might well have happened. If it had taken
place, Cambodia would have had the dubious distinction of
severing diplomatic relations with two of the three Global
Powers.

A policy of drift is fatal. Confrontation with a Global Power
should be avoided; but if it becomes unavoidable, it should be
faced instantly and firmly. Delay or irresolution inevitably
results in piecemeal compromises, which in turn injure the
national interests of the small nation. However, before resort-
ing to confrontation, every reasonable effort should be made to
avoid a direct diplomatic clash by insulating the points of
conflict. In striving for such an arrangement as a first measure,
the state concerned will not be compromising its stand. On the
contrary, it will prove that the cause is so dear to it that, even
against the opposition of a Global Power, it will be pursued
more practicably in accordance with the situation, instead of
getting bogged down in sterile controversy, resulting in mounting tension without the national aim being achieved. Once a
working accommodation is achieved by the insulation of
points of conflict, persuasion and indirect efforts will become
more effective. It is safer and more prudent to avoid a head-on
collision with a Global Power. It is wiser to duck, detour, step
aside, and enter from the back door. It is futile to try to win over
or implore a Global Power to change its policies by continued
direct efforts on the plea of justice or alignment. Reminders of
services rendered in the past are of no avail. Neither cringing nor
sycophancy, neither sentiment nor argument, carry any weight
in such dealings. The simple fact of the matter is that, in the
long run, a Global Power is not likely to be outwitted, so it is

better for a small nation to take a realistic attitude and evolve both policy and strategy on rational rather than on subjective lines. The objectives of such a nation will stand a better chance of being realized by the application of indirect pressure exerted by the collective voice and solidarity of the smaller nations of Asia, Africa, and Latin America (now known as 'the Third World'), together with diplomatic pressures from those Global Powers and quasi-Global Powers whose interests are in accord. By combining the support of such Powers as can give it with the support of the underdeveloped nations, the state concerned can bring about situations which make it imperative for the Global Power in question to modify its position in its own independent interest. It is largely by the compulsion of these outside forces that the state concerned can bring about a change in the Global Power's attitude on the points of difference. In other words, it is necessary for small states to maintain a dialogue on their conflicting interests with all Global Powers, irrespective of their positions; to do all within their resources to influence them without getting entangled to the point of interference and ultimata.

With the points of conflict set aside, a small nation can have normal and friendly dealings with Global Powers on all matters except on the actual issues of conflict. This would enable the State in question to enjoy a rational latitude in maintaining better relations with those Global Powers whose interests co-incide with its own. In such an event, the Global Powers whose interests are in opposition cannot take exception to that state's more cordial relations with the Global Powers whose interests are in accord. Nor would this justify the Power with whose interests its own are in conflict in interfering in or adversely influencing the small state's national interests, since no preconditions would be made for normal relations.

How should smaller nations regulate their relations with the two Communist giants? There are many doctrinaire and political reasons for the Sino-Soviet schism. One is perhaps to be found in the contending interests of the Global Powers. Had it not been for the dispute between China and the Soviet Union, it might not have been impossible for the Communist World, represented by the Soviet Union and China, and the Capitalist World, represented by the United States, notionally to divide the world into different spheres of influence. In such a dispensation, China would have acquired a secondary position. Unlike Britain, however, China is not reconciled to playing a secondary role. The threat of the partition of the world has, therefore, been averted by the equality that China seeks with the United States and the Soviet Union. This political fact of life, this global clash at the summit, is of supreme significance to the rest of the world. The external policy of any country must be based on a realistic assessment of the current power conflicts. These add tension to tension, but also offer opportunities, which small powers can ill afford to ignore, for the protection of their own vital interests and, indeed, sovereignty.

The conflicts of the Global Powers are not only ideological but also a struggle for hegemony. The original confrontation between the United States and the Soviet Union has now been succeeded by that between the United States and the People's Republic of China, with the Soviet Union occupying an intermediary position. In this balance of power between the three titans, the Soviet Union, willy-nilly, appears to be getting pushed into a midway position, at once advantageous and hazardous. Because its claims to leadership of the Communist countries, especially those of eastern Europe, are based on ideology, only at the cost of international Communism can the Soviet Union allow its ideological differences with the People's Republic of China to reach a point of no return. The widening breach between the two Powers has weakened the Soviet position in eastern Europe, where complex and profound changes are taking shape, without affecting China's influence in Asia. Failing an ideological *rapprochement* with China, the Soviet leadership will be caught between twin pressures: menaced from the west by the liberals and harassed on the east by the Chinese traditionalists. Neither can the Soviet Union allow its *détente* with the United States to reach a point leading to the Soviet Union's identification with the Captain of Capitalism. In drawing this conclusion the importance of ideology is not being overstated. On occasion, national considerations might well supersede ideological considerations, but this will never be admitted; on the contrary, as these trends become more apparent, greater lip-service might be paid to ideology as an instrument for achieving national objectives. Thus, although the Soviet

Union retains a modicum of flexibility in its relations with the
United States and China, sometimes taking a position more in
accord with the United States and sometimes, though rarely
now, with China, it cannot pursue this path indefinitely and
make it a feature of its permanent policy, without jeopardizing
its position in world affairs.

Although the People's Republic of China and the United
States have become arch-antagonists, and the Vietnam war
has brought them to the brink of an international war, it should
not be assumed that their relations will always remain in a state
of hyper-tension. The United States' interests are world-wide,
like those of the other Great Powers, but its primary interests
remain in Europe, where it has to compete with the vital
interests of the Soviet Union. China's main dispute with the
United States, apart from the Vietnam war, is over the future
of Taiwan. There would not be much argument as to whether
Germany or Taiwan is more important to the security of the
United States. Were it to come to a choice or a show-down,
undoubtedly it is Germany and the future of Europe which
would get priority from the Americans. From defence considerations alone, the loss of Taiwan would not endanger the
United States' security interests as vitally as the loss of Germany.
In a number of Asian states in the Pacific region, the United
States has an array of defence facilities encircling China and is
in physical possession of a string of strategic islands facing the
coastline of China. Moreover, there is the Seventh Fleet which
would continue to patrol the Pacific and other Asian waters.
Thus, the loss of Taiwan and other off-shore islands would
not be of paramount importance to the strategic requirements
of the United States' interests in Asia. Similar advantages are
not available in Europe in comparable measure and variety.
America has to rely primarily on her ground forces and nuclear
missiles.

The conflicting interests of the United States and the Soviet
Union are not confined to Europe. In terms of importance, the
Middle East takes second place. There, as in Europe, the United
States' chief rivalry is not with China, but with the Soviet
Union. The strategic Middle East, with its oil wealth, the Suez
Canal, and the problem of Israel, is again more important to
the United States than the future of Taiwan. Both in terms of

interest and commitment, the Middle East—as the crossroads between Africa, Asia, and Europe—takes precedence over south-east Asia in America's global objectives. Following the Second World War, the United States took the place of Britain and France in this region. The Persian Gulf area produces 27 per cent of the world's petroleum and has proven global reserves of 60 per cent. American firms have a gross investment in the region of $2·5 billion. There is nothing comparable in respect of American interests to be found in the south-east Asian peninsula. On the other hand, the Soviet Union has continued to extend its influence in the region by supporting the Arab cause against Israel and in rendering massive economic and military assistance to the Arab states, beginning with its dramatic participation in the construction of the Aswan Dam.

The stakes of the Soviet Union and of the United States are undeniably very great in the Middle East and second only to their interests in Europe. So far as the United States is concerned, Israel is both a subject of international concern and an in-tensely important domestic problem. So great are American interests in this region that, although the Soviet Union's own interests are considerable, it nevertheless modified the position it took at the start of the crisis in the Middle East war for fear that the United States would protect its stakes at whatever cost. Notwithstanding the short-term American successes in the war of June 1967, in the Middle East as in Europe, the Soviet Union and the United States are vying with each other for supremacy.

There is little doubt that the Soviet Union was embarrassed in the recent Middle East conflict. The setback then suffered had to be put right; hence Premier Kosygin's hurried journey to the General Assembly, President Podgorny's quick visits to Cairo, Damascus, and Baghdad, and the immediate replenishment of military equipment to Arab States. These were part of a deter-mined effort by the Soviet Union to retrieve its position not only in the Arab states, but in the world generally.

It would be a dangerous over-simplification to assert dogmat-ically that, on account of the prevailing area of understanding between the United States and the Soviet Union in Europe and because of the setback to the Soviet position in the Middle East, the *détente* between the two Global Powers has now be-come a permanent fact of international life. Even if the Soviet

Union should want such an understanding, the contradictions in the international situation simply do not permit it.

The United States has no territorial disputes with the People's Republic of China, whereas there are territorial differences between the Soviet Union and the People's Republic of China. Another important factor in causing a change in the existing Global Power positions is the stark fact that, militarily speaking and in terms of industrial and technological development, it is the United States and the Soviet Union which are evenly poised. These have attained such fearful military power as to be capable not only of destroying each other but the rest of the world with them. China has not yet attained a similar degree of military prowess. The balance of terror between the United States and the Soviet Union places China in a position to tilt the scales in favour of the one or the other. If China were to be destroyed by the United States, the vacuum thus created would endanger the Soviet Union's security. It therefore follows that despite the differences between China and the Soviet Union, it is not in the Soviet Union's basic national interest to carry its disputes with China to the ultimate end. Similarly, despite the United States' *détente* with the Soviet Union and its antagonism to China, because of American and Russian rivalry in Europe and the Middle East and because of the territorial and ideological differences between the Soviet Union and China, it is not in the United States' national interest to carry its struggle against China to a point of no return. It is therefore conceivable that, despite the sharp and seemingly irreconcilable differences between the United States and China and all that has recently happened in the Middle East to display the United States–Soviet Union *détente*, a situation may still arise in which China and the United States jump over existing obstacles and arrive at a working arrangement uncongenial to the Soviet Union. Equally, circumstances may throw a bridge across the gulf dividing China and the Soviet Union and compel them to re-assert their unity against the Anglo-American Powers in the face of one reversal after another, beginning with the failure to hold the Second Afro-Asian Conference and culminating in the Middle Eastern debacle. These reverses are made all the more grave by the shadow that Vietnam casts over Sino-Soviet interests.

The international milieu is in a state of flux as the power centres shift and the East–West ideological struggle is partially overtaken by the North–South polarization, which arises from the appalling economic disparity between the rich and the poor nations. The rigid polarization of the last decade is giving way to a process of decentralization of power. The speed of change is more rapid than we imagine and it is accelerating. Great changes are taking place everywhere and the greatest of these are in Asia. In this fluid state of affairs it would be fatal to be dogmatic about the future course of international events. At present the United States is engaged in a conflict—just stopping short of war—with China; such a situation cannot last for ever. Judging by existing trends, which point towards a collision course, the likelihood of a change in the wind of events appears to be remote. It would be safer to predict that the understanding between the two Super-Powers, dramatically demonstrated by the Middle East conflict and tenaciously pursued by President Johnson in his summit discussions with Premier Kosygin at Glassboro, will continue to grow at the cost of China and in favour of a settled international *status quo* policed by the Soviet Union and the United States. This might well happen; but in the exciting kaleidoscope of power politics all possibilities have to be taken into account. The intriguing thing about international politics is that it contains no law which rules out any kind of change resulting from the interplay of objective interests.

More and more people are coming to believe that the United States and the Soviet Union are now engaged in ending the dangerous phase of the cold war. They do not always appreciate, however, that a diminution of the confrontation might precipitate more serious problems and lead to a series of armed conflicts in different parts of the world. The cold war has persisted for over two decades mainly because the Soviet Union and the United States tacitly renounced war as a means of settling their disputes. The world has become acquainted with the traditional pattern of the cold war and its limitations. People feel increasingly secure in the knowledge that it will not explode into open violence. The waning of the cold war in one form or another could generate genuinely dangerous situations. Into the void might step a Great Power unafraid of the consequences of modern warfare as a means of ending exploitation. To prevent this, the established Great Powers, weary of war, might make compromises and admit reforms ending neither in the perpetuation of the unjust *status quo* nor in the capitulation of genuine interests. But as long as nations exploit one another, as long as there is dictatorship and suppression of civil liberties, as long as people are denied their rights and the poor are plundered, the cold war will remain and might even culminate in a real war between the Great Powers, between one ideology and the other. Oppressed people will never abandon their search for a redeemer and if none is found to assume the mantle, the people in bondage will redeem themselves and achieve an egalitarian order free of domination and want, tyranny and exploitation. In the last analysis, it is better to live under the familiar shadow of the cold war than to experience the nightmare of racial war towards which we appear to be moving inch by inch.

There was a time when the Soviet Union and the United States were the world's principal adversaries. Ten years ago few would have anticipated their present relationship. Similarly, it cannot be ruled out that a time will not come when the United States and China will have to seek a *modus vivendi*. If this does not happen, it could precipitate the destruction of the world, or, at any rate, of Asia. There are no permanent enemies. The existing conflict between the United States and China must one day give way to sanity. From the mid-thirties to the mid-forties Nazi fascism was the cause of conflict. From the mid-forties to the mid-fifties the Soviet Union and the United States were locked in their cold war. From the mid-fifties we have witnessed the increasing antagonism between the United States and China, an antagonism that cannot last for ever. To be more cautious than Professor Toynbee, who dared to forecast that history would take an unprecedented turn, I am willing, at least, to predict that there will be a turn in events in the middle seventies. If the past is any index to the future, it is doubtful whether the intensity of the United States–China confrontation can endure beyond the seventies. As in the case of the confrontation between the United States and the Soviet Union, the China–United States confrontation is not likely to end in victory and defeat, but in the erosion of the sharp edges of conflict.

We may draw the lesson that the smaller nations must not be carried away by the present Global Power differences and indulge in excesses on behalf of one against the other so as irretrievably to undermine their own futures. They should, rather, uphold just causes by working for de-colonization and by offering resistance to aggression, uninfluenced by the position of the Global Powers. The smaller nations would do well to assume an increasingly non-committal position in the Global Power antagonisms. It would be myopic for them to identify themselves completely with one Power against another. This does not mean that, in furtherance of its national interests, a small nation should not take a position more in accord with one Great Power than another; but it certainly means that the small state should avoid taking predetermined positions on all international issues on the basis of identification with one Great Power as against another, for the sake of fleeting material benefits or because its regime in power believes that it is being propped up by a Power without whose support it would be liquidated by its own people.

In practical terms, the smaller states should evolve a policy to maintain normal bilateral relations with all the Global Powers, devoid of interference, in a perfectly understandable gradation based on enlightened national interest. If these relations are to be productive and consistent, the terms of association should be such as not to favour one against the other in strictly ideological matters or in defence commitments; otherwise, their relations will assume the character of multilateral under-takings. As Great Powers have global obligations, it is difficult to have bilateral relations with a Great Power in matters of defence without becoming involved in a chain reaction result-ing in multilateral obligations. Such agreements cut across the benefits of bilateralism and lead to conflicts with other Global Powers. The terms of bilateral relations should in no way vitiate the scope and content of similar relations with other Global Powers. In other words, under no circumstances should bilateral relations assume the character of multilateral obligations, as would happen if the terms of the different bilateral relations were to conflict on fundamental issues and become irreconcil-able.

It is essential for the nations of the Third World to continue to develop friendly bilateral relations not only with the Global Powers but also with the quasi-Global Powers such as Britain, France, and Germany. France, invested with the additional degree of power which stems from the possession of nuclear weapons, maintains the confidence of the French-speaking states of Africa. Her voice commands respect in other African countries and among the states of Asia and Latin America. In the latest crisis in the Middle East, France has regained her position among the Arab states and made atonement for the wrongs she inflicted on them during the Suez war of 1956. That the France of 1968 is not that of 1956 was acknowledged by President Nasser when he praised General de Gaulle for his country's constructive role in the Middle East conflict. France has acquired for herself a special position not only in Europe but also among the nations of the Third World. By virtue of her far-sighted foreign policy, she has developed closer understanding with the Soviet Union and the People's Republic of China. Her correct appraisal of the Vietnam war and the general situation in Asia has further enhanced her stature, while her external policies have opened new opportunities for a more progressive change in the international equilibrium. By her unwavering support of the principles of self-determination, courageously implemented against her metropolitan interests in Algeria, she has left a salutary impression on the nations of the Third World.

Franco-German collaboration, which began promisingly under Konrad Adenauer, has since received some reverses. If this collaboration is consolidated, it could become a powerful factor in Europe and be a bastion of peace for the rest of the world. At present, West Germany, as a component part of a divided state, seeks the unification of its nationhood. For this supreme objective, and for its defence, it is excessively dependent on the United States. Its foreign policy has therefore become immobile. It lives in constant fear of betrayal by its principal ally, as any basic understanding between the Soviet Union and the United States must be largely to the disadvantage of the Federal Republic of Germany. Since the formation of the coalition Government, under Chancellor Kiesinger, there is again a revival of the movement towards France and an approach to Europe more in accord with the thoughts of General

c

de Gaulle. It would, however, be premature to expect any major departure in German foreign policy before the General Elections scheduled for 1969, unless some fundamental understanding is reached between the United States and the Soviet Union at what the Federal Republic would regard to be its cost.

Great Britain has now ceased to be a powerful force in Asia, but she continues to play an important marginal role in support of the United States' global interests. Her provocative 'East of Suez' policies have caused much avoidable trouble in west and south-east Asia. After the Middle East conflict, it is doubtful whether the United Kingdom will ever again be able to assert herself 'East of Suez'. She will have to make the choice between the welfare of her people and the overlordship of others.

The Commonwealth has passed the point of mutual benefit. It has become a vestigial institution and the sooner it is decently and voluntarily dissolved, the better it will be for Britain and for the Asian and African nations of the Commonwealth. All the collective frustrations of Asia and Africa and the inability of the Commonwealth to find a release for these feelings reflect themselves in the relations with Britain and cause unnecessary complications. As inter-Commonwealth disputes have no outlet within the institution, they mount one on top of another to increase misunderstandings. Today, relations between Britain and South Africa are better because they are on a bilateral basis. When South Africa was in the Commonwealth, Britain's relations with that country were strained because of the tensions which the multilateral combination of the Commonwealth generated against it. Not only would Britain's bilateral relations with all the members of the Commonwealth improve, but the voluntary liquidation of the Commonwealth would permit Britain to enter Europe unburdened by past legacies and would free the states of Asia and Africa to play a more natural and meaningful role within their own continents and in the cause of Afro-Asian solidarity. There would be no anomalous overlapping of obligations and responsibilities, which only increase individual and collective burdens and dilute the natural aspirations of the peoples of Asia and Africa. Britain's place is in Europe and the sooner Britain finds it the better it will be for Europe and for world peace. Britain began from Europe and to Europe she must now return. At present her tentacles are spread far beyond her capacity. She must readjust herself to the call of the times and reorientate her policies, primarily in respect of Europe. The decision to reduce British military commitments in Asia is a step in that direction.

Underdeveloped nations always find it a difficult and anxious business to make adjustments in their relations with the Global Powers. It is much easier for them to co-ordinate their policies in their mutual interest in improving their bargaining positions *vis-à-vis* the Global Powers and to strengthen their solidarity. It must remain a constant endeavour of the underdeveloped nations to increase their mutual co-operation, which, being a relationship between equals, is incapable of causing damage to the vital interest of any member of the community.

Afro-Asian solidarity must be pursued resolutely within and outside the United Nations. There are bound to be reverses like the failure to hold the second Afro-Asian Conference and the crisis in the United Nations itself. So extensive a movement for freedom and justice cannot fail to encounter innumerable impediments, but the challenge should strengthen the resolve for unity, which is sure to emerge in the course of time. Once the lean years of the United Nations are over, that organization can, in fulfilment of its early promise, still become the vehicle of progress and the shield of protection for the underdeveloped nations of the Third World. At present the United Nations is besieged by crises, its chief difficulty being the test it faces in the Middle East. Some people believe that if it fails to pass this test, it will die like the League of Nations, but it has been pronounced dead before and has managed to survive. Once it surmounts the present troubles and reorganizes itself, it should be able to reassert its influence and offer an effective forum to the nations of Asia, Africa, and Latin America for influencing the course of international events and setting into motion the power of public opinion in support of their legitimate struggles. If, however, it sinks under the weight of present problems, there will emerge another United Nations, more faithful and vigorous in the service of oppressed peoples and exploited nations. Thus, there will always be an international forum for the expression of truth and for the defence of justice. The world cannot be turned into the real estate of the Super-Powers. With all its weaknesses, the United Nations is an improvement on the League of Nations, and if it disintegrates, a more efficacious world forum will come into being on its ruins.

As the weapons capable of destroying whole continents are brought nearer to technical perfection, it becomes all the more imperative for the underdeveloped nations of Asia, Africa, and Latin America both to understand each other more comprehensively and in a spirit of solidarity, and to work actively for a better understanding between all developed and underdeveloped nations. The cliché that the world is shrinking is none the less true; for the speed of communications has rendered distance of no consequence in the calculation of decisions affecting international peace or leading to international war. The impact of important decisions is felt beyond the frontiers of any single country or people. The reverberations of such decisions today extend to the four corners of the world.

The North–South polarization of the underdeveloped nations' struggle for a better economic relationship with the developed nations makes it incumbent on the underdeveloped nations to articulate their common objectives in order to strengthen their collective bargaining capacity. The North–South struggle, however important it may be for the future welfare of the underdeveloped nations, is overshadowed by the East–West polarization, which has the power of inciting ideological passions. This East–West polarization is the expression of the will to dominate the economic and social conditions of the world and therefore carries within itself the menace of a universal holocaust capable of reducing civilization to a heap of ashes. It is therefore necessary for the continents of Asia, Africa, and Latin America to arrive at a new and equitable understanding with the continent of Europe, in accordance with the requirements of contemporary events.

After the havoc wrought by the Second World War, Europe was sick and exhausted. Today it shows every sign of rejuvenation and its once war-weary people appear to be destined for a happier and fuller life. The nations of East and West Europe, having laid aside the implements of war, are now engaged in an effort at greater co-operation. The softening of bipolarity has introduced greater flexibility in East–West relations and created new political and economic fluidity. This encouraging movement for European solidarity has aroused fresh hopes of finding a solution to the remaining European problems. The chances of breaking the stalemate seem better under European auspices free from external intervention. To what extent the two Super-Powers would permit, or be able to control, the increasing co-operation between the nations of Eastern and Western Europe remains to be seen; what is clearly discernible is that the mood for such co-operation within Europe exists. This makes it all the more necessary for the nations of the Third World to make a fresh approach to the Europe that is emerging.

A new kind of relationship is evolving between Europe and Asia. In the past, on account of European domination of Asia, the two continents had more differences than mutual ties. It was inevitable that, in a relationship based on inequality and exploitation, discords should mount between the peoples of these two regions. With the passing of the age of physical domination, a new depth has come in the relations between Europe and Asia. In the phase of altering relationships, the peoples of Asia and Europe are beginning to explore the similarities that unite them rather than the differences that divide them. Absurd notions like that of the 'White Man's Burden' and the moral responsibility of a 'superior race' to civilize the 'barbarians' are exercising a diminishing influence on the mentality of Europeans and their behaviour towards Asia. Vestiges of old attitudes still remain, but are fast disappearing. The emphasis is now shifting to the common denominators and to the importance of the geographical contiguity of Asia and Europe. It must not be forgotten that the major migrations to Europe took place from Asia; thus there is a certain intermingling of races and cultures. Both continents have been the cradles of civilizations and from both have spread religious thought, philosophy, science, and political ideas. Both continents have been the scene of terrible wars and destruction. Europeans and Asians alike should therefore be the more deeply conscious of the need to establish a just international peace. The future holds a bright promise for greater collaboration between Asia and Europe in making the world a better place to live in. This opportunity should be seized imaginatively and put to good use. The years ahead will reveal the depth of common interest. It will become more apparent when the Great Powers redefine and readjust their objectives in the changed context of development in Europe and Asia; when hegemonies meet with united resistance; when fresh ground is broken in science and the general composition of events flowing from economic and social conditions.

The importance of a universal, intercontinental understanding and association is in no way diminished by the assertion that geography continues to remain the most important single factor in the formulation of a country's foreign policy. If a nation is incapable of adjusting itself to its next-door neighbour, it will find it much more difficult to arrive at an understanding with nations situated far away. A nation's maturity and flexibility in international relations is born of the maturity and flexibility of its behaviour towards its immediate neighbours. Indeed, international co-operation would be greatly facilitated if all neighbours were able to arrive at a good understanding among themselves. Territorial disputes, which are the most important of all disputes, arise among neighbours and create tension in relations between neighbouring states. As with individuals the most complex international situations arise in the conduct of relations between states with common frontiers. Both by virtue of their proximity and the wide scope of their mutual relations the foreign policies of neighbouring states not only tend to intensify and aggravate differences between themselves, but they also present a varied range of day-to-day problems. It is in this sphere, therefore, that a nation manifests its general ability. Although in this century distance does not efface ethnic and spiritual bonds, nevertheless geography, in its physical sense, remains the most potent factor governing the importance of relations between neighbouring countries. Many relations can be changed or influenced, but not the reality of the presence of a geographical neighbour. This is a permanent factor in the shaping of foreign policy.

In the conduct of foreign policy, the benefits of cultivating good relations with countries in general, can often be neutralized by a country's failure in relations with its neighbours. A nation's political philosophy and its social system are subject to modification and change. Technology, material resources, and political structures are all susceptible to change, but the physical facts of geography are immutable. At any given time, the foreign policy of a country must therefore represent a synthesis of variable factors with those that are fixed. Thus, in the difficult task of formulating foreign policy and in facing international pressure as well as the aggressive intent of adversaries, account needs to be taken of a variety of highly complex factors, such as a nation's political philosophy, its economic system, its cultural traditions, and its geographical location.

This chapter has attempted to present in simple terms a very complicated problem, and its purpose will have been served if it has succeeded in demonstrating that the changed political situation in the world—the emergence of three Global Powers and the struggle for the domination of men's minds all over the world—requires great vigilance on the part of statesmen of the smaller nations who control the destinies of their people. Their method of approach to the Global Powers in the conduct of their foreign policy and their solidarity among themselves will ultimately determine whether the nations they guide will retain their independence and self-respect in the world of tomorrow.

CHAPTER 3

American Attitudes towards Partition and Indian Neutralism

Situated in Asia and being an underdeveloped country, Pakistan has to adjust its foreign policy to the world situation on the basis of progressive, enlightened national interest infused with a desire for universal peace and justice. Pakistan is an ideological state or, to be more precise, a state with an ideology. To the Muslims of the sub-continent it is a God-inspired country; the expression of the idea of justice and equality translated into reality by the process of self-determination. Pakistan has specific international responsibilities in accordance with its nature; it must of necessity take up such a position as will permit it to contribute to the fullest extent in the discharge of its inner obligations, to the consolidation of world peace and the realization of equality amongst all peoples and nations; and will at the same time permit it to deal with its own problems.

Fired by the zeal to end domination and to achieve equality, the Muslims of the sub-continent struggled for a separate state and were successful in attaining Pakistan. Although there are some who still regret the division of the sub-continent, it is quite evident that without partition none of the Muslim peoples of pre-Partition India would have been able to protect the values they hold to be supreme and regard as indispensable to a world freed from domination.

Practically the whole of India had been united in ancient times during the reign of Emperor Asoka, and later at the apogee of the Mughal Empire when Aurangzeb's fiat prevailed from one end of the sub-continent to the other. In both cases it was an imposed unity. Polyglot India remained a rich diversity of conflicting cultures held together by imperial orders. It was not a case of culture and unity flowing from the fountainhead of a single nationality. Indeed, the concept of nationality or nationhood, such as we know it, evolved much later. The British, too, gave unity to India which, like that of Asoka and Aurangzeb before them, was imposed on the land. This later imperial unity was remarkably heterogeneous in nature, for parts of the country were directly ruled and parts were ruled by princes bound to the British Crown by treaties. Even so, it was only during the British period that the concept of nationality began to germinate in the consciousness of Indians. In a period of a hundred and fifty years it could not be expected to take unshakeable root. British rule, however, did arouse a feeling of national consciousness, not in one single indivisible entity, but in two powerful different communities, each with its own distinct culture, religion, and aspirations.

After the British conquest of the sub-continent, it remained their jealously guarded preserve for over a century and a half. Except for the French and the Portuguese who held minor possessions, the coastline of the sub-continent was sealed off from other Powers. At one end, the Himalayas reached the skies and ensured the isolation of the country as effectively as the oceans. Whatever traditional contacts existed beyond the Himalayas were broken by the conquerors to complete the isolation of 'the brightest jewel in the crown'. The British saw India as a land of mystery and superstition, of strange contrasts, of religions and warring chieftains. It was the heaviest burden the white man carried in his mission to civilize the world. Having eliminated the other colonial powers, the British went ahead alone to complete their humanizing mission. The war of 1857, called 'The Indian Mutiny', led to the barbaric suppression of the spirit of the people. The reprisals were so severe that for succeeding decades the writ of imperial Britain remained undisturbed by any popular uprising. The Khilafat Movement was the next genuine universal revolt against British domination. This Muslim movement was adroitly exploited by Mr. Gandhi for launching the demand of the Congress for National Independence. For many years the Congress, under the able leadership of Mr. Gandhi, held the field. The struggle for independence and the Indian National Congress became synonymous terms. It was much later that Mr. Muhammad Ali Jinnah, under the banner of the Muslim League, launched the movement for self-determination of the Muslims of the sub-continent.

The British were hostile to the Muslim demand for partition. Mr. Jinnah, known as Quaid-i-Azam, had to face the dual opposition of the British and the Indian National Congress in his struggle to attain Pakistan. The age of colonialism with its prescription of 'divide and rule' was giving way to the era of neo-colonialism, which required the enforcement of the new formula of 'unite and rule'. The changed conditions and the corresponding demands of neo-colonialism required the unity of the sub-continent for the maximum exploitation of larger markets and for defence against the incursions of Communism. It was feared that to divide the sub-continent would be to 'divide and lose'; that access to the vast raw-material markets would be impeded, and the defence of the region weakened against the age-old Russian ambition to control the sub-continent and the Indian Ocean. On the basis of this appreciation, the British resisted partition to the end.

If the British had left India 'united' as one state, there would be today four or five national states in the sub-continent. The choice was not between leaving India as one united country or divided into two, but between leaving India divided as two nations, or letting it burst into fragments of not fewer than four or five states. The creation of Pakistan has contributed to the crystallization of an Indian nationhood. Were it not for the hatred for Pakistan prevalent in India, India would have found it extremely difficult to restrain her polyglot provinces from breaking away. As it is, despite the animus against Pakistan, India has been just about able to maintain her unusual degree of unity. This is a factor of great significance and one that foreign Powers would do well to remember in their endeavour to bring about an effective reconciliation between India and Pakistan. Instead of creating an indivisible sub-continent to face 'the Communist menace' more effectively, the splinters might fly off in all directions to destroy the objectives of certain Global Powers. In plain language it means that the effort to absorb Pakistan might lead to the end of India as it stands today. Such a disintegration would immediately invite all the disastrous consequences the West is seeking to avoid by pressing Pakistan to confederation with India.

People who do not understand the ethos of Pakistan and whose concept of nationhood is fixed on stereotyped territorial considerations have missed the spirit that inspired the Pakistan Movement, the great struggle for equality in which the Muslims chose freedom to unity. Such people are apt to rush to judgement on the economic and defence viability of Pakistan, indeed on its very existence. Looking at the country from a distance, and without an adequate knowledge of its foundations, they conclude that it would have been infinitely more advantageous to their global interests if the sub-continent had remained together. They fail to appreciate that it is the existence of Pakistan, equally poised as an indivisible nation at either end of the sub-continent, that keeps India in one piece. If the evenly balanced scales of Pakistan tilt one way or the other, India's equilibrium cannot remain unaffected. How much more disagreeable would this not be for those foreign interests which look askance at the partition of the sub-continent into two nations?

For a fuller assessment of the problems of Pakistan and its domestic situation it is necessary to revert to the evolution of events in the sub-continent and of the Great Powers' approach to the two countries both before and after Independence. An appropriate starting point would be the attitude of those Powers to the sub-continent at the moment when India and Pakistan were at the threshold of freedom.

Germany had already been destroyed and France, humiliated by her defeat, was not immediately in a position to regain her global importance. With the assistance of the Allied Powers, she sought to retake her colonies in south-east Asia and in Africa. China had been badly mauled by Japan; nevertheless, Chiang Kai-Shek had taken an interest in the independence of India but had been rebuffed by the British, who regarded his efforts as unwarranted interference in the affairs of their Empire. The Generalissimo and his wife visited India and held discussions with Indian leaders, after which, on 12 February 1942, Mr. Nehru spoke of the affinities between the ancient Indian and Chinese civilizations and outlined a plan for a federation embracing India, China, Persia, and other smaller countries, with the object of maintaining their independence and contributing to world peace. Mr. Churchill described Generalissimo and Madame Chiang Kai-Shek's visit to India in the following words:

The object of their journey was to rally Indian opinion against

Japan and to emphasize the importance for Asia as a whole, and for India and China in particular, of Japanese defeat. The Indian Party leaders used the occasion to bring pressure upon the British Government through the Generalissimo to yield to the demands of Congress.

The War Cabinet could not agree to the head of a foreign State intervening as a kind of impartial arbiter between representatives of the King Emperor and Messrs. Gandhi and Nehru.[1]

Mr. Churchill prevailed upon the Generalissimo 'not to press the matter at a time when unity was imperative'.

The Soviet Union had emerged as a victorious Great Power, but it had virtually no contact with the sub-continent and its knowledge of the political situation was incomplete. Moreover, it was more concerned with the future of Eastern Europe and Germany. Such interest as it had in Asia was largely confined to the northern parts of Iran, the territories of Japan, and to the fortunes of a China beset by an internal power struggle between the Chinese Communist Party and the Kuomintang. This does not mean that the Soviet Union was not interested in India, but rather that there were other matters demanding prior attention. The first essential was to face the challenge of the cold war, the focal point of which was Europe. Britain had won the war but come out of it greatly diminished in strength. She continued for a while to be the spokesman of the West more for historical reasons than for those of power realities. Much before the end of the war, it was apparent that the United States would assume the responsibility for the leadership of the West, with Britain falling behind. As early as 1913, Mr. Walter H. Page, the United States Ambassador to Great Britain, wrote to President Wilson: 'The future of the world belongs to us. . . . These English are spending their capital. . . . Now what are we going to do with the leadership of the world presently when it clearly falls into our hands? And how can we use the English for the highest uses of democracy?'[2] In 1920 an American writer, Ludwell Denny, concluded in his book entitled *America Conquers Britain*: 'We were Britain's colony once. She will be our colony before she is done: not in name, but in fact. Machines gave Britain power over the world. Now better machines are giving

---

[1] *The Second World War*, 1951, vol. 4, p. 183.
[2] Burton J. Hendrick, *The Life and Letters of Walter H. Page*, 1923, vol. 1, p. 144.

America power over the world and Britain. . . . What chance has Britain against America? or what chance has the world?'

After the Second World War there could be no doubt of the ascendancy of the United States. However, for some years America leaned on Great Britain for advice and diplomatic initiative, and for a period of time Britain became to the United States what Greece had been to Rome. In this period of transition, Britain was liquidating its Empire in India. The United States had no definite contact with the Indian situation. It relied heavily on Britain for information and advice. It is true that the United States was keen to see an independent India and, on occasion, irritated the British by pressing them to proclaim Indian independence at an early date. It would not be accurate to say that the United States was opposed to partition as such, but it may certainly be said that the United States preferred a united India and was sympathetic to the Congress demand for an undivided India. America also agreed with the British assessment of the dangers to Western interests of a partitioned India, but was not sufficiently familiar with the details and nuances of the Indian political situation to take a definite position on partition. The United States was well aware of the country's political and geographical importance and hoped to see China and India built up as two strong Western bastions.

Many overtures were made to the leaders of the Indian Congress in the period of the early and mid-forties and, on 21 July 1941, it was announced that representatives were to be exchanged between the United States and India. In December 1941, during Mr. Churchill's visit to Washington, Mr. Roosevelt discussed the Indian problem with him at length. Later, at the end of February 1942, President Roosevelt instructed Averell Harriman to sound Mr. Churchill on the possibilities of a settlement between the British Government and the Indian political leaders. In response to Mr. Harriman's visit, Mr. Churchill wrote to President Roosevelt on 4 March 1942:

We are earnestly considering whether a declaration of Dominion Status after the war, carrying with it, if desired, the right to secede, should be made at this critical juncture. We must not on any account break with the Muslims, who represent a hundred million people, and the main army elements on which we must rely for the immediate fighting. We have also to consider our duty towards

32 to 40 million Untouchables and our treaties with the Princely States of India, perhaps 80 millions. Naturally we do not want to throw India into chaos on the eve of invasion.[1]

Later, the rapid Japanese advance in south-east Asia prompted President Roosevelt to press Mr. Churchill harder on the question of independence for India. Mr. Churchill has described the United States' pressure in the following words:

The United States had shown an increasingly direct interest in Indian affairs as the Japanese advance into Asia spread westwards. The concern of the Americans with the strategy of World War was bringing them into touch with political issues, on which they had strong opinions and little experience. Now that the Japanese were advancing towards its frontiers, United States Government began to express views and offer counsel on Indian affairs. . . .[2]

On 11 March 1942 President Roosevelt sent his views on the Indian question to Mr. Churchill. Citing the example of the origins of the Government of the United States, he suggested

the setting up of what might be called a temporary Government in India, headed by a small representative group, covering different castes, occupations, religions and geographies—this group to be recognized as a temporary dominion Government. The principal thought of President Roosevelt's scheme was that 'it would be charged with setting up a body to consider a more permanent Government for the whole country'.[3]

During the Cripps Mission to India Colonel Louis Johnson, President Roosevelt's Special Envoy to India, who remained closely in touch with the deliberations of the Mission, said in a press interview on 22 April 1942, *inter alia*:

Only by throwing back the invader can India hope to take her place among the great States of the World. We in the United States are watching with profound interest the development of India and China, because we realize that in Indian and Chinese hands lies the destiny of Asia; the union of these two great Asiatic blocs in the cause of liberty may well be the greatest political development of ten centuries.[4]

It was during this time that President Roosevelt sought to establish direct contact with the leaders of the Indian National

---

[1] Churchill, op. cit., p. 185.   [2] ibid.   [3] ibid., p. 189.
[4] *Keesing's Contemporary Archives*, vol. IV, 1940–3, p. 5299.

Congress and sent an invitation to Mr. Nehru to visit him in Washington, but the Congress Leaders were so infuriated at the non-acceptance of their total demands by the Cripps Mission that Mr. Nehru declined to visit Washington. On 26 April 1942 Mr. Gandhi made a prophetic observation:

If the British left India to her fate, as they had to leave Singapore, non-violent India would not lose anything. Probably the Japanese would leave India alone. The American troops must go with the British. We know what American aid means. It amounts in the end to American influence, if not American Rule, added to British.[1]

Again, on 17 May Mr. Gandhi wrote that 'America could have remained out of the war, and even now she can do so if she divests herself of the intoxication her immense wealth has produced.'[2] A week later he declared: 'Leave India in God's hands, in modern parlance, to anarchy, and that anarchy may lead to internecine warfare for a time or to unrestrained dacoities. From these a true India will rise in place of the false one we see.'[3]

It might be mentioned that many still believe that once the demand for partition was accepted, it would have been better to divide the country and remove those elements of foreign supervision which inevitably remained in the civil service, the armed forces, the police, and the judiciary. The withdrawal of foreign elements might have led to greater bloodshed, but it would have drawn a clearer and more natural line between India and Pakistan. It would not have tormented the people of Pakistan with iniquitous boundary awards and, above all, the fraud perpetrated on the people of Jammu and Kashmir by an Instrument of Accession aided and abetted by a Head of State who was a foreigner and who viewed the problems from the vantage point of his country's interest.

In December 1946 at the time of the Indian Congress and Muslim League meetings in London, Mr. Dean Acheson, Acting Secretary of State of the United States, wrote:

I am confident that if the Indian leaders show the magnanimous spirit which the occasion demands, they can go forward together on

---

[1] R. Coupland, *Indian Politics*, 1943, p. 290.
[2] ibid.   [3] ibid.

the basis of the clear provisions on this point contained in the Constitutional Plan proposed by the British Cabinet Mission last spring to forge an Indian Federal Union in which the elements of the population will have ample scope to achieve their legitimate political and economic aspirations.[1]

A few months before the emergence of India and Pakistan, the Truman Doctrine was proclaimed and this was followed, on 21 June 1947, by the Marshall Plan to bolster the nations of Western Europe against the threat of the Soviet Union. The principal purpose of the United States' foreign policy, to contain Communism, had taken definite shape. The Truman Doctrine was designed to assist Greece and Turkey against Soviet penetration and internal Communist subversion. The Marshall Plan was conceived to prevent Communist penetration into Western Europe and, in 1949, the North Atlantic Treaty Organization was established to strengthen the defence of Western Europe against the Soviet Union's military threat. In this period of tense and ferocious confrontation with the Soviet Union Mr. Richard P. Stebbins wrote that 'The partition of the sub-continent between these two mutually antagonistic nations had disrupted its economic and politico-strategic unity and aggravated beyond measure the task of governing its discrete fragments.'[2]

The views of one or more writers, however eminent, do not constitute the policy of a government, but what can be inferred without fear of contradiction is that Western interests required a united India in order to face the Soviet Union more effectively and to retain large markets for economic exploitation. However, in spite of external machinations, the Muslim demand for self-determination became so irresistible that neither the British nor the Indian National Congress could prevent the birth of Pakistan, the embodiment of the principle of self-determination.

At the time when India and Pakistan became independent, the old British Empire was crumbling. The colonial system of direct territorial domination was being replaced by economic and financial controls in conjunction with the maintenance of a large number of military, naval, and air bases in every con-

---

[1] *Indian Annual Register*, 1946, vol. 2, p. 88.
[2] Richard P. Stebbins, *The United States in World Affairs, 1950*, 1951, p. 317.

1 The author with Chairman Mao Tse-Tung in Peking, March 1963

tinent, intensive armament preparations and a network of military alliances. This was the beginning of the hegemony of the Global Powers. The young states of India and Pakistan came into contact with the United States for the first time in this unfamiliar pattern of Great Power politics. In those days the main objective of America's Asian policy was to obtain the participation of India and China in the promotion of the United States' interests in Asia. Immediately after Independence President Truman extended an enthusiastic invitation to Prime Minister Nehru to visit the United States, and Pandit Nehru when he went was given a splendid reception. During the course of his visit, and subsequently, considerable efforts were made by the United States Administration to establish a special relationship with India. When in 1949 India agreed to remain in the British Commonwealth, *The New York Times* hailed this decision as 'an historic step, not only in the progress of the Commonwealth but in setting a limit to Communist conquests and opening the prospect of a wider defence system than the Atlantic bloc'.[1] In the autumn of that year Prime Minister Nehru told the United States' Congress that India would not be neutral in a war 'for freedom and justice', and the *New York Times* wrote with appreciation that 'Washington's hopes for a democratic rallying point in Asia have been pinned on India, the second biggest Asiatic nation, and on the man that determines India's policy— Prime Minister Jawaharlal Nehru.'[2] Again, in August 1950, the same paper called Nehru 'in a sense the counter-weight on the democratic side to Mao Tse-Tung. To have Pandit Nehru as ally in the struggle in Asiatic support, is worth many divisions.'[3]

China, the other pillar in the edifice of the United States' Asian policy, was removed by the Communist revolution when, on 1 October 1949, Mao Tse-Tung emerged victorious. This event had a powerful impact on India, which, as a result of the changes in China, began to play an ever more independent role in world affairs. India sought to maintain a balanced policy between China, the Soviet Union, and the United States, but this the United States interpreted as being contrary to its interests and favourable to the global aims of China and the

[1] K. P. Karunakaran, *India in World Affairs Feb. 1950–Dec. 1953*, 1958, p. 238.
[2] ibid.   [3] ibid.

Soviet Union. On 17 October 1949 Prime Minister Nehru declared:

Inevitably she [India] had to consider her foreign policy in terms of enlightened self-interest, but at the same time she brought to it a touch of her idealism. Thus she has tried to combine idealism with national interest. The main objectives of that policy are: the pursuit of peace, not through alignment with any major power or group of powers, but through an independent approach to each controversial or disputed issue.[1]

Although by the middle of the fifties it had become fairly evident that India was determined to pursue an independent neutralist foreign policy, the United States persevered in its endeavour to extend its influence in India, notwithstanding repeated disappointments. In December 1950 the United States signed a 'Point Four' agreement with India and, in October 1951, Mr. Chester Bowles was sent to that country to appraise the Indian situation and to offer generous assistance for India's First Five Year Plan. In 1951 a mutual Defence Assistance Agreement was signed between India and the United States, which enabled India to receive certain military assistance from the United States without any of the corresponding obligations that devolved on aligned states. Another Agreement was signed by the two countries, at the beginning of 1952, for the establishment of an Indo-American Technical Co-operation Fund, with further advances over a period of five years, totalling $250 million.

While taking advantage of American unilateral overtures, India remained steadfast in her independent foreign policy. On the question of the Japanese Peace Treaty, the Government of India sent a note to the United States Government announcing its inability to subscribe to that treaty. In reply to this note, on 26 August 1951, the United States expressed regret that India would not participate in the treaty and felt aggrieved at her decision to make a separate peace treaty with Japan. When, in February 1953, President Eisenhower announced the United States' policy of 'de-neutralizing' Formosa, President Rajindra Prashad criticized it, and Mr. Nehru condemned it as the 'military mentality' of seizing countries.

By this time increasing influence was being exerted by the

[1] Karunakaran, op. cit., pp. 238–9.

United States on the countries of what was called the 'defensive perimeter'. Especially after the Korean war, American policy in south-east Asia was governed on the one hand by the global conception of presidential doctrines and the 'containment' policy, and on the other, by the concept of the 'defensive perimeter', under which Japan in particular emerged as the central concern of United States policy in the Pacific. After China was lost to America, the original conception of India and China as the twin pillars of the United States' south-east Asia policy was reconstituted, with Japan replacing China.

Pandit Nehru, however, stoutly resisted every attempt to put India in this subservient position—to the regret of many eminent American political commentators. Richard P. Stebbins, for example, wrote:

The refusal of the Indian Government to accept this country's interpretation of the Far Eastern crisis and to endorse our various protective actions against Communist China had caused lively annoyance in Washington and for the time being destroyed the possibility of co-ordinated action with Asia's leading non-communist Government. India's policy mirrored with painful clarity the distrust of the West, the insistence on the rights of Asia's re-born peoples.[1]

On 28th August 1951, *The New York Times* wrote editorially under the title 'The Lost Leader':

Jawaharlal Nehru is fast becoming one of the great disappointments to the post-war era . . . to the West, he seemed (a few years ago) a logical champion of a free democratic, anti-communist Asia, and the India he directed was the obvious candidate for the leadership of Asia . . . instead of seizing the leadership of Asia for its good, Nehru turned aside from his responsibilities, proclaimed India's disinterestedness and tried to set up an independent Third Force India, suspended in mid-air between the two decisive movements of our day—the Communism that Russia heads, and the democracy of which the United States is the champion.

Mr. Raymond Cartier has written:

There is certainly not a country in the world where America is more suspect as a Nation and the American more despised as an individual than in India. Nehru has never ceased to obstruct every

[1] *The United States in World Affairs, 1950,* 1951, p. 315.

American effort to organise the defence of Asia but Nehru in this
case merely interprets the distrust and animosity of his people.[1]

In *The United States in its World Relations*, Nelson M. Blake and
Oscar T. Barck, say of the Asian participation in SEATO:

The prestige of the alliance suffered particularly from the unwil-
lingness of India, Burma, Ceylon and Indonesia to participate.
These nations that had recently won their independence from Britain and the Netherlands looked with suspicion on SEATO as a cover
for the perpetuation of colonialism. . . . American relations with India
were clouded by mutual suspicions and misunderstandings. Prime
Minister Jawaharlal Nehru was determined that India should play a
fully independent role in world affairs and refused to commit his
country to either the Communist or anti-Communist blocs. . . .
Indian representatives in the United Nations were accused of playing
the role of Communist stooges. Unable to anchor its Asiatic defence
lines on India, the American State Department tied itself by
alliance and military aid programmes to India's rival, Pakistan—
thereby still further embittering Indian-American relations.[2]

Russell H. Fifield maintains that

At the time of the Manila Treaty negotiations [1954], all the
powers directly concerned were eager to have as wide an Asian
participation as possible. India, Burma, Ceylon and Indonesia
would have been welcomed partners but they chose to stay outside.
In fact, India and Indonesia—and to a lesser extent Burma and
Ceylon—were highly critical of the Manila Conference, accusing it
of creating tensions and dividing nations.[3]

In *India and America* Sunderlal Poplai and Phillips Talbot wrote
that 'American military help and political alliance have gone
to Pakistan only and not also to India solely because India has
declined such help and association';[4] and to conclude, as I
began, with the view of Richard P. Stebbins:

Had the United States been less firmly committed to its world-
wide strategic programme, or had India been somewhat less un-
sympathetic to American views on the 'cold war', this country
might have hesitated to take a step which threatened to complete
the breach of confidence which had been developing with the

[1] Raymond Cartier, 'Why Does the World Hate America?' in Robert A. Gold-
win, ed., *Readings in American Foreign Policy*, New York, 1959, p. 598.
[2] 1960, pp. 749–50.
[3] *South-East Asia in U.S. Policy*, 1963, p. 121.   [4] 1959, p. 70.

largest democracy in Asia. As things stood, however, Indian-American relations were already in a condition that made many Americans doubtful whether it was really possible to continue taking Indian susceptibilities into account.[1]

Despite the many allurements held out by the United States to India, the growing disenchantment with that country began to manifest itself in a number of pronouncements by important American officials and political leaders. On 12 February 1951 President Truman stated:

I recognize that there are important political differences between our Government and the Government of India in regard to the course of action which would most effectively curb aggression and establish peace in Asia. However, these differences should not blind us to the needs of the Indian people.[2]

India's refusal to be inveigled by the United States in the cold war forced the United States to change its attitude towards the sub-continent. Senator Knowland, leader of the majority party in the American Senate during the years 1952–4, was reported to be of the view that 'neutralist nations like India do not deserve the same military or economic aid as our active allies, or an equal place at the Conference table'. In August 1953 the United States Government came out openly against the inclusion of India in the proposed political conference on Korea. Secretary of State Dulles made no secret of his displeasure at some of the actions of the Indian Government in the international field. Opposing India's representation at the conference, he said that exclusion from such a conference was the price she should pay for her policy of neutralism. According to *United States News World Report* of 4 January 1954, Vice-President Nixon, 'tended to favour military aid to Pakistan as a counter-force to the confirmed neutralism of Jawaharlal Nehru's India'.

It will be seen from these few but pertinent citations of official and non-official opinion that the United States began to look for alternatives only when it came to the distressing conclusion that India's independent neutralist policy had taken root, and that she was unwilling to collaborate in the United States' Asian strategy. Just as, after the victory of the Chinese

---

[1] *The U.S. in World Affairs in 1953*, 1954, pp. 312–13.
[2] *Keesing's Contemporary Archives*, vol. VIII, 1950–2, p. 11538.

Communists, Japan had replaced China as one of the pillars of its Asian policy, so Pakistan was to replace an India unprepared to give its allegiance to the United States' global objectives.

However, despite the feeling that India was being disobliging, the United States continued to entertain the hope that in the course of time she might change her outlook; and so nothing untoward was done to displease her. Regardless of resentment caused in the United States over India's violent opposition to the proposal to establish a Middle East Defence Organization, in May 1953 Mr. Dulles promised to continue American aid to enable India to implement her Five Year Plan. In making this commitment, he paid tribute to India's efforts in the United Nations to bring an end to the hostilities in Korea.

Summing up the United States' attitude towards India at this period, Blake and Barck write:

> Despite these recriminations, neither India nor the United States could afford a serious rupture, since each needed the other. Attempting an ambitious programme of economic development to combat the nation's desperate poverty, India wanted American economic aid and technical assistance. And the American Government, in turn, realised that to cut off aid to India would be to abandon a crucial front to the Soviet Union, already showing an eagerness to send equipment and technicians into underdeveloped countries as a means of enlarging its political influence.[1]

Neither during the darkest period of United States–Indian relations, nor during the brightest phase of the United States–Pakistan relations, did the United States take a stand as an ally of Pakistan in the Indo-Pakistan disputes. It rewarded the most outrageous Indian provocations with massive economic assistance to that country, and accepted the complete identification of Pakistan with its interests without allowing these factors to determine the whole range of assistance to either country. When the United States decided to give military assistance to Pakistan, President Eisenhower expressed his country's willingness to give aid to India also. In a letter delivered to Prime Minister Nehru on 24 February 1954 he wrote:

> I send you this personal message because I want you to know

[1] *The U.S. in its World Relations*, 1960, p. 750.

about my decision to extend military aid to Pakistan before it is public knowledge, and also because I want you to know directly from me that this step does not in any way affect the friendship we feel for India. . . . What we are proposing to do, and what Pakistan is agreeing to, is not directed in any way against India. I am confirming publicly that if our aid to any country, including Pakistan, is misused and directed against another in aggression I will undertake immediately . . . appropriate action, both within and without the U.N., to thwart such aggression. I believe that Pakistani-Turkish collaboration agreement is sound evidence of the defensive purposes which both countries have in mind. . . . We also believe that it is in the interest of the free world that India should have a strong military defence capability, and have admired the effective way in which your government has administered your military establishments. If your government should conclude that circumstances require military aid of a type contemplated by our mutual security legislation, please be assured that your request would receive my most sympathetic consideration.[1]

Although the United States' decision to extend military assistance to Pakistan caused misgivings in India, Mr. Nehru remained steadfast to non-alignment and, on 1 March 1954, rejected President Eisenhower's offer in the following words: 'You are, however, aware of the views of my Government and our people in regard to the matter. Those views and policy which we have pursued after most careful thought, are based on our desire to help in the furtherance of peace and freedom. We shall continue to pursue that policy.'[2] On that very day, the Prime Minister of India vehemently criticized the United States' military assistance to Pakistan and termed it as 'intervention' in Indo-Pakistan affairs. He observed that the United States was attempting to 'dominate' Asia and announced that the Indian Government was no longer prepared to accept the United States' Observers in Kashmir as neutrals. In so far as President Eisenhower's offer was concerned, he declared that 'In making this suggestion, the President has done less than justice to us or to himself. If we object to military aid being given to Pakistan, we would be hypocrites and unprincipled opportunists to accept such aid ourselves.'[3] The Mutual Security and Assistance Agreement concluded, on 19 May 1954, between

---

[1] *Keesing's Contemporary Archives*, vol. IX, 1952–4, p. 13461.
[2] ibid., p. 13462.   [3] ibid.

Pakistan and the United States was followed by a Conference of eight countries at Manila in September 1954 and an agreement was reached on creating SEATO. Although Cambodia, Laos, and South Vietnam were barred by the Geneva Armistice from entering into such alliances, the United States included these countries within the area to be protected against an 'armed attack'.

One year later the Baghdad Pact was concluded, and re-named CENTO after the Iraqi *coup d'état* in July 1958. In conformity with the United States' policy of the 'defensive perimeter' and 'containment', which required enlisting key-states into alliances and appeasing the others with economic support outside the alliances, the United States chose not to make an outright commitment to the Baghdad Pact in order to mollify the fears of those non-Communist states who considered the Pact to be an 'imperialist thrust' in the region. Pakistan was separately covered by another commitment by virtue of the Montreal Defence Pact of 1956. Again, early in 1959 the United States signed bilateral agreements of co-operation with Turkey, Iran, and Pakistan, which were designed to strengthen further the military aspects of CENTO. In the preamble to the Pakistan–United States Bilateral Agreement of Co-operation of March 1959, the United States undertook to preserve the 'independence and integrity of Pakistan'.

Although, by this time, Pakistan had veered fully into the American sphere of influence, the considerations prevailing in the United States' economic aid policies remained unaffected. During the aid allocation for the fiscal year 1954–5, Mr. Dulles stated that the largest single item—$85 million out of $307,400,000—was earmarked for India, and urged Congress to support this request in spite of disagreements on foreign policy between New Delhi and Washington. After praising Mr. Nehru as a 'leader dedicated to the democratic form of Government', he went on to say:

> We believe that India's great effort to achieve economic progress should be supported. We should remember that among free nations there is room for diversity of views. We should not let our wish to help the people of India to develop their nation be swayed by any temporary difference, however important. It is essential that we continue to help, if for no other reason than to serve our enlightened

self interest. It would be a tragic day for us if the confidence which people have in their democratic institutions should fail.[1]

On 10 March 1956 Mr. Dulles stated in a Press Conference in New Delhi that he saw no reason why the supply of American arms to Pakistan should lead to an arms race in the sub-continent. He went out of his way to extend a reassurance to India:

There can be every confidence on the part of India that there will be no use of these armaments in any aggressive way against India. Pakistan knows that if that should happen, there will be a quick ending of its good relations with the US, and that, under the UN Charter, the USA would support India if she became a victim of any armed aggression.[2]

In a special foreign aid message on 31 March 1959, President Eisenhower declared that collective security would become more rather than less important as we moved into the age of missile weapons. The friendly nations in whose territory many of these weapons would be deployed, he said, needed the continued assurance of American help to their forces and defence. Some 250 bases 'in the most strategic locations, many of them of vital importance', had been made available for the use of American forces by other members of the free world. 'Dollar for dollar', the President insisted, 'our expenditure for the mutual security programme after we have once achieved a reasonable military posture for ourselves, will buy more military security than far greater additional expenditures for our own forces.'

---

[1] *Keesing's Contemporary Archives*, vol. IX, 1952–4, p. 13744.
[2] ibid., vol. X, 1955–6, p. 14841.

CHAPTER 4

India seeks American Support against China

With the United States' policy well grounded on the concept of military alliances, it was not surprising that the warmth of the United States–Pakistan relations continued to increase during the late fifties, reaching their highest point just when India's relations with China suddenly deteriorated in late 1958 and early 1959. United States–Pakistan relations endured some slight tremors during the Ladakh clashes, and some more severe ones when the Sino-Indian border dispute began to intensify. In these developments the United States saw a great new opportunity—that of realizing its long-cherished ambition to spread its influence over India.

1959 marked the end of one era and the beginning of another. Mr. Manzur Qadir was then Foreign Minister of Pakistan and I was in New York leading Pakistan's delegation to the United Nations General Assembly. In a letter addressed to him from there, I gave warning that the conflict in Ladakh would give rise to many changes in the sub-continent. The Dulles era had come to an end and a new situation was evolving for which the inflexible diplomacy of 1945–58 would no longer be suitable. The conditions of the forties and early fifties had altered radically. Europe was changing and there were changes in the Soviet Union; the world was moving away from the dogmas of Dulles to the spirit of Camp David. These and other developments in Asia and elsewhere called for a reorientation of the United States' foreign policy. The changes came sooner than expected by Pakistan. The regime, which was closer to the United States than any previous Government, was not psychologically prepared to accommodate itself to the changes caused by the rigidity of American post-war policies.

The magnitude of the change can be measured, in economic

terms, by the fact that at 30 June 1959 American economic aid to India in the twelve years since Independence was officially valued at over $1,705 million, including $931 million in agricultural commodities and some $774 million in other forms of assistance. As against this amount, as much as $4 billion were given in economic aid to India during 1959–63.

In May 1959 Senator Wiley Smith, who had then returned from a tour of south-east Asia, gave the following testimony to the Senate Foreign Relations Committee:

> There is no doubt of the fact in my mind from talking to Nehru and his close advisers, that there was some concern about the Red Chinese and their operations on the border. . . . From the standpoint of the United States, it is a hopeful sign that the Indian Government is becoming somewhat alarmed over Red Chinese operations and is conscious of that fact, as explained to me by some of the leaders, that Red China has made great forward strides in industrialization under a totalitarian system, whereas India has moved much more slowly because of its intention to act only under democratic processes, and with full concurrence of the Indian Legislature.

Perhaps for the first time military aid to Pakistan was seriously criticized in these hearings, although it was concluded that for five years it should continue at the current level, but emphasis was laid on the importance of building up Indian strength against China. The document entitled *United States Foreign Policy*, compiled by the Senate Foreign Relations Committee in August 1959, set out the following objectives:

1. Use of bilateral aid to stimulate co-operation among the developing countries of Asia.
2. Re-examination of the role of local military forces and US bases in Asia in relation to US strategic, political, and economic objectives.
3. Inclusion of the countries concerned to undertake regional accords against Communism. India and Pakistan were specifically mentioned in this connection.

While changes in the United States' policies were taking shape, American commentators were for the first time critical of the system of alliances and Pakistan's inclusion in them. In *The United States in World Affairs 1959*, Mr. Richard P. Stebbins said: 'In effect, the formation of SEATO in 1954 divided South and Southeast Asia politically in much the same way that the Baghdad Pact was to divide the Middle East a year later.'[1] Correspondingly, the need for support to India and other non-aligned countries began to be increasingly felt in the United States. Mr. Stebbins goes on to say:

> Many students of Asian affairs felt that there was even more urgent work to be accomplished in this second field—the building of healthy national societies—than in the field of military defence to which the United States had felt compelled to give its main attention through most of the 1950s. Action in this latter realm could at least be conducted over a much broader front, since even the neutral countries in the area were usually willing to accept outside help for non-military purposes if it was obtainable 'without strings' and on terms compatible with their own dignity. All of these countries, from Afghanistan to the Philippines, were aware that their progress as modern states was being seriously retarded by unfavourable economic and social conditions. . . .

> Many Western observers considered the successful implementation of India's successive five year economic plans to be of crucial importance not only for India itself but for the whole cause of Asian independence. . . .

> With a population now estimated at 415 million and increasing by seven million a year, India's need for accelerated economic development was so great that the United States could scarcely resent its acceptance of aid from Communist as well as free world quarters, especially when the Indians had given so many proofs that they did not intend to allow their independence to be compromised. . . .[2]

The border skirmish of November 1959 in Ladakh established the seriousness of the Sino-Indian differences and prompted President Eisenhower to undertake a tour of Asia on which he wanted to discuss regional problems with Mr. Nehru against the background of the Sino-Indian border controversy. The President expressed satisfaction at the outcome of these discussions and hoped for an era of better understanding between the United States and the largest democracy in Asia. In January

[1] 1960, p. 282.
[2] op. cit., pp. 283, 284, and 297.

1961 Senator John F. Kennedy became President of the United States. He was among those liberal Democratic Senators who had doubted the wisdom of President Eisenhower's policy of establishing a rigid system of alliances against Communism. Such a system seemed to him not only outmoded but likely to diminish Western influence over non-Communist nations. As a Senator, Kennedy had already shown his unhappiness over what he considered to be the neglect of India, which, in his estimation, occupied a position of pivotal importance in the American strategy of containing Communism in Asia. He elaborated these views in the Senate on 25 March 1958:

Mr. President, let us recall again the profile of the Asian Continent. India, with its nearly 400 million souls, and China, a country in the neighbourhood of 600 million. Let us not be confused by talk of Indian neutrality. Let us remember that our nation also during the period of its formative growth adopted a policy of non-involvement in the great international controversies of the nineteenth century. Nothing serves the ultimate interests of all the West better than the opportunity for the emergent uncommitted nations of the world to absorb their primary energies now in programmes of real economic improvement.

This is the only basis on which Asian and African nations can find the political balance and social stability which provide the true defence against Communist penetration. Our friendships should not be equated with military alliances or 'voting the Western ticket'. To do so only drives these countries closer to totalitarianism or polarizes the world in such a way as to increase rather than diminish the chances for local war.

In considering the economic future of India, we shall do well to recall that India has passed the point of economic take-off and is launched upon an effort which will by the end of the century make her one of the big powers of the world, with a population of just under one billion and capable of harnessing all the resources of modern science, technology, and destruction. No greater challenge exists in the future than the peaceful organization of a world society which includes not only the wealthy industrial States of America, Western Europe, and Russia, but also powerful new industrial states in Asia, Latin America, Africa and the Middle East. How these states emerge from their period of economic transition will not only colour but quite likely caste the historic setting of the next generation. This question was recently set in these words by

Professor W. W. Rostow before the Senate Foreign Relations Committee:

> Shall these new powerful States emerge to maturity from a totalitarian setting, their outlook dominated by bitter memories of colonialism and by memories of painful transition made without help while the rich West stands by, concerned only with the problems of defence? Or shall these States emerge from a democratic setting, built on human values, shared with the West, and on memories of shared adventure in the decisive periods of transition?

The answer to this question will not be long in the making if we do not act now and over the next few years, for India, the most important of all the non-committed States, has entered its formative period. A successful Indian programme is important at least as such for the example it can set for the economic future of other under-developed countries as for its own sake. The United States, Western Europe, and Japan have it in their power to make a demonstration that the democratic process is a persuasive method of creation, not frustration. . . . India today represents as great a hope, as commanding a challenge, as Western Europe did in 1947—and our people are still, I am confident, equal to the effort.[1]

In his conversations with John Fischer, the following question and President Kennedy's answer are revealing:

> Q: Do you think it was a mistake for us, under Mr. Dulles' administration, to try to force a good many of these underdeveloped countries into military pacts with us?
>
> KENNEDY. . . . I would say that Mr. Dulles was probably more successful in Germany, really, than he was in some of these other areas. The Aswan Dam refusal, the concept of the Baghdad Pact, which was his, and the Eisenhower Doctrine, which is being rejected really in every country—all these, I would think, are unhappy monuments to Mr. Dulles in the Middle East.[2]

However, before the 1959 Sino-Indian clash in Ladakh, Senator Kennedy was not prepared to support India at the cost of alienating Pakistan. This is borne out by the following extract from a speech he delivered before the Senate on 25 March 1958:

our special and valued treaty relationships and military pacts with Pakistan do not make possible such an international effort for India.

---

[1] John F. Kennedy, *The Strategy of Peace*, 1960, pp. 157–8.
[2] ibid., p. 219.

I myself have for some time investigated the possibility of devising a programme which would jointly serve the needs of India and Pakistan.

I have regretfully concluded that the current political cleavages between India and Pakistan do not allow such a programme. . . . The choice is not one between India and Pakistan. Our responsibility is to aid each in its basic development programmes. I hope the time is not far off when these types of multilateral efforts can be adopted to aid the economic growth of Pakistan.[1]

But in his speech in California on 1 November 1959, when Sino-Indian border tension was rife, Senator Kennedy decided to give all-out support to India:

Whatever battles may be in the headline, no struggle in the world deserves more time and attention from this Administration—and the next—than that which now grips the attention of all Asia: the battle between India and China. . . .

And that is the struggle between India and China for the economic and political leadership of the East, for the respect of all Asia, for the opportunity to demonstrate whose way of life is the better. . . .

It should be obvious that the outcome of this competition will vitally affect the future of all Asia—the comparative strength of Red and free nations—and inevitably the security and standing of our own country. India's population is larger than the total population of the continents of Africa and South America combined. Unless India can compete equally with China, unless she can show that her way works as well as or better than dictatorship, unless she can make the transition from economic stagnation to economic growth, so that it can get ahead of its exploding population, the entire Free World will suffer a serious reverse. India herself will be gripped by frustration and political instability, its role as a counter to the Red Chinese in Asia will be lost and Communism will have won its greatest bloodless victory. . . .

It is not enough that we participate on a crash basis, for temporary relief. We must be willing to join with other Western nations in a serious long-range programme of long-term loans, backed up by technical and agricultural assistance—designed to enable India to overtake the challenge of Communist China. . . .

We want India to win that race with Red China. We want India to be a free and thriving leader of a free and thriving Asia. But if our interest appears to be purely selfish, anti-communist, and part of the Cold War—if it appears to the Indian people that our motives

[1] ibid., p. 154.

are purely political—then we shall play into the hands of Communist and neutralist propagandists, cruelly distort America's image abroad, and undo much of the psychological effect that we expect from our generosity.[1]

With regard to military pacts, he reiterated on 9 February 1959 that they

provide no long-term solutions. On the contrary, they tend dangerously to polarize the Middle East, to attach us to specific regimes, to isolate us very often from the significant nationalist movements. Little is accomplished by forcing the uncommitted nations to choose rigidly between alliance with the West or submission to international Communism. Indeed, it is to our self-interest not to force such a choice in many places, specially if it diverts nations from absorbing their energies in programmes of real economic improvement and take-off.[2]

On 14 June 1960 Senator Kennedy attacked the policies of the Eisenhower Administration in the following terms:

To be sure, we have, in 1960, most of the formal tools of foreign policy: we have a defence establishment, a foreign aid programme, a Western alliance, a disarmament committee, an information service, an intelligence operation and a National Security Council. But we have failed to appraise and re-evaluate these tools in the light of our changing world position. We have failed to adapt these tools to the formulation of a long-range, co-ordinated strategy to meet the determined Soviet programme for world domination—a programme which skilfully blends the weapons of military might, political subversion, economic penetration and ideological conquest. We are forced to rely upon piecemeal programmes, obsolete policies and meaningless slogans. We have no fresh ideas to break the stalemate in Germany, the stalemate over arms control, the stalemate in Berlin and all the rest. We have as our grand strategy only the arms race and the cold war. . . .

So let us abandon the useless discussions for who can best 'stand up to Khrushchev' or whether a 'hard' or 'soft' line is preferable. Our task is to rebuild our strength, and the strength of the free world—to prove to the Soviets that time and the course of history are not on their side, that the balance of world power is not shifting their way—and that therefore peaceful settlement is essential to mutual survival. Our task is to devise a national strategy—based

---

[1] John F. Kennedy, *The Strategy of Peace*, 1960, pp. 142–3.
[2] ibid., p. 122.

2 The author with President John F. Kennedy in the White House,
October 1963

not on eleventh-hour responses to Soviet-created crises, but a comprehensive set of carefully prepared, long-term policies designed to increase the strength of the non-communist world.[1]

When Mr. Kennedy became President of the United States he was in a position to put his plans into practice. His country's relations with India and Pakistan were now to be governed by the philosophy of 'containing' Communism through a ring of economically strengthened, free, and neutral nations, supported by United States' military power against Communist encroachment. The emphasis on greater economic aid was designed to provide markets for United States' goods in order to maintain pro-West links with the recipient countries. The value of military bases and alliances was greatly reduced by spectacular advances made in military technology. These developments, among others, were responsible for the shift in emphasis from military support to further economic collaboration. The ability 'to fire a missile from the United States, under our control, in case of a threatened attack or if a vital interest of ours was endangered', had the virtue of reducing dependence on allies who, on account of the American military bases in their territories, tended to compromise the United States' freedom of action in the service of its interests in international relations. Shortly after his inauguration President Kennedy took a number of decisions which soon began to affect the United States' relations with India and Pakistan. His admiration for Nehru was revealed when, in his address to a joint session of Congress, he declared: 'I can vividly recall sitting where you sit now . . . the undimmed eloquence of Churchill, the soaring idealism of Nehru, the steadfast words of de Gaulle'.[2]

Corresponding changes in India's attitude were seen in the United Nations, where she collaborated with the United States on the Congo issue and opposed the Soviet Union's campaign against Secretary-General Dag Hammarskjöld. American grievances against India's past actions in the United Nations were fast beginning to disappear and, indeed, she was encouraged to take initiatives on questions concerning Africa and Asian affairs. Simultaneously, negotiations were undertaken to

[1] ibid., pp. viii and ix.
[2] *Dawn* (Karachi) Editorial, 24 February 1961.

E

provide India with massive economic assistance for her new
Five Year Plan in the form of Long Term Development Fund
loans at very low interest rates repayable over a forty- to fifty-
year term. President Kennedy was reported to be ready to ear-
mark nearly one third of the proposed new Development Fund
for India. Vice-President Johnson was made to undertake a
tour of Asia on a mission to establish a new equilibrium between
the United States and India and other non-aligned States. During his visit to India he declared: 'I am confident without
reservation that India and the United States will continue to
build a friendly and a wholesome relationship. This I can
assure you is very much welcome on the part of America. Our
President John F. Kennedy's high regard for India and India's
leadership needs no reiteration beyond the presence here of
Ambassador Galbraith.' Senator Fulbright, Chairman of the
United States Senate Foreign Relations Committee, observed
that it was for India and other nearby countries to play a more
active military and economic role in the defence of the area.
On 6 May 1961 Mr. Averell Harriman, the United States'
Roving Ambassador, was reported to have told Mr. Nehru that
it was the view of the United States' Administration that certain
neutral countries of Asia should underwrite the neutrality of
Laos.

George E. Jones, a staff reporter for *United States News and
World Report*, wrote that 'Jawaharlal Nehru, Prime Minister of
India, is turning out to be a top favourite of the Kennedy Administration among statesmen of the world.' He disclosed that
the proposed massive economic aid to India was designed to
link India and Nehru securely to the West. Indian behaviour,
he stated, 'was also supporting this thesis as Nehru "lined up"
against the Soviet attempt to unseat Dag Hammarskjöld as
Secretary-General of the United Nations. He moved Indian
troops into the Congo at a time when the United Nations' force
there seemed about to collapse. In Laos, he supported British
moves for a cease-fire and urged Khrushchev to accept them.'

On 18 May 1961 Krishna Menon, attending the 14-Nation
Conference on Laos in Geneva, joined the Western powers in
objecting to the veto provision sought by the Soviet Union in
its 'peace plan'. The previous month, twenty-four hours after
attacking United States' 'intervention' in Cuba, Nehru con-

veniently changed his tune—calling Mr. Kennedy 'dynamic'
and suggesting that 'there might be two sides to the Cuban
story'. He also said that 'at present, President Kennedy and his
top advisers say that Nehru can become a firm friend of the
West. That, they say, would bring large dividends to the United
States in India and other under-developed parts of the world.'
This growing demonstration of confidence was again made in
June 1961, when the Indian Ambassador to Washington, Mr.
M. C. Chagla, on the eve of his return to India said:

> When I came here neutralism was distrusted and suspected. Today
> it has become respected . . . the switch in American policy is so
> great that America now wants neutral states in Africa and Southeast
> Asia . . . and take economic aid. What we have been proposing for
> a long time—long-term loans in support of social justice and not
> propping up reactionary Governments—this is now completely
> accepted here, at least by the White House as demonstrated in
> President Kennedy's proposals.[1]

As well as President Kennedy and some of his advisers, there
were many other leading Democrats who expressed themselves
enthusiastically in favour of India. Many of them began to
question military assistance to Pakistan. Mr. Chester Bowles,
for instance, said that 'it was bad arithmetic to alienate 360
million Indians in order to please 80 million Pakistanis who are
split in two halves and divided by 1,000 miles of Indian territory'.
Senator Fulbright observed that the 'American military aid to
Pakistan was much excessive and that this policy forced India,
because of the apprehension caused by Pakistan, to deviate
funds from economic development'.

The turn of events in the sub-continent rekindled not only
all the old passions for India but also the known prejudices
against partition. Voices were again heard criticizing the
division of the country on the anachronistic concept of religion
and questioning the whole viability of a country the two parts
of which are separated by a thousand miles of hostile territory.
The cold arithmetic of Mr. Chester Bowles, who calculated his
conclusions in terms of population and territorial length and
breadth, was subjected to renewed scrutiny. Nehru's trouble-
some policies and the irritation generated by his non-alignment

[1] *Dawn* (Karachi), 4 June 1961.

were forgotten, as was the fidelity with which Pakistan attached itself to the United States' interest. Undoubtedly, substantial economic and military assistance was rendered to Pakistan, but it was not without an adequate *quid pro quo*. Pakistan had undertaken to stretch her defence commitments against the Communist Powers without a categorical assurance with regard to her security against India. She had incurred the hostility of the Soviet Union, which openly supported Afghanistan and India against Pakistan. The policy of alignment also damaged Pakistan's image in the United Nations, strained her relations with neighbouring Islamic Arab states, and drove her towards isolation in the community of Asia and Africa. The changes in the sub-continent and on the Himalayan frontiers had erased with a single stroke both the services of Pakistan and the antagonisms against India.

On 6 June 1961 the Consortium pledged a total of $2·2 billion aid to India out of which the United States alone pledged $1·45 billion, which was more than half the total. According to *Time* magazine of 9 June 1961, the United States' eagerness to give aid to India had 'startled' its aid partners in the Consortium. As against this, Pakistan's relatively meagre requirement of $945 million was slashed by the same Consortium. Simultaneously, it was heard that military aid would also be granted to India after adequate provision had been made in the Mutual Security Act for aid to neutrals. Defence Secretary McNamara was reported to have testified before the Senate Foreign Relations Committee that all the four conditions of the Mutual Security Act, which required a recipient nation 'to ally itself politically and militarily, with the free world against the Communist bloc' were to be removed as they were 'not appropriate in agreements for essential military assistance to the newly independent nations'. He further asserted that India had achieved greater stability than her neighbour, Pakistan, due to her 'able political administrative traditions', and suggested that the conditions of the Security Act be removed in the case of India. This departure from established policy was yet another sign of the new philosophy of aid, tailored to suit India's special requirements. These events necessitated a meeting between President Kennedy and President Ayub Khan, who went to the United States in July 1961 to make renewed efforts to restore the relationship of confidence between Pakistan and the United States. The hesitant manner in which aid was now extended to Pakistan was described by President Ayub Khan, on 9 July 1961, in a television interview in London:

Now in respect of India, the United States made a special effort with the other contributing countries to persuade them to match the United States' effort. The United States went out of her way to bequeath a billion dollars as their contribution at a time when the Indian plan was not even worked out.

In our case, all sorts of objections were raised. Some were genuine while some were, to my mind, spurious—the sort of things which are designed to put off a caller. There did not seem to be a real effort to recognise the situation. And I don't think the United States made any special effort. If they had expected the other contributing countries to match the United States' effort, they should have told them that there will be this call too, and that the United States expects them to do this, that or the other.

All I say is that USA did not make any real effort in this regard. But let us hope that this performance will be improved next time.[1]

The result of the discussions between the two Presidents, as revealed in their joint communiqué and President Ayub Khan's statement after the meeting, can be summarized as follows:

1. Pakistan's alliance with the United States had been strengthened and misgivings in the mind of President Ayub had been removed;
2. President Kennedy had agreed to raise the question of Kashmir with Mr. Nehru and impress upon him the necessity of bringing about a just and peaceful solution of the problem;
3. Pakistan had been assured that its military problems would not be made difficult, and if and when arms aid was given in this region Pakistan would be consulted. It was further assured that military aid would not be given in this region unless there was a very good cause for giving it;
4. The United States was not selling any armaments to India;
5. Pakistan's economic-aid requirements would be fully met;

[1] Field Marshal Mohammad Ayub Khan, *Speeches and Statements*, vol. IV, July 1961–June 1962, p. 6.

6. The United States would assist Pakistan financially and technically in solving problems of waterlogging and salinity.

President Ayub Khan expressed satisfaction at the repaired relations, but as subsequent events showed, President Kennedy had made some accommodation to Pakistan's needs chiefly because the Sino-Indian conflict of 1959 had not yet been extended. There was speculation on whether the differences would be resolved or become wider. In 1961, during President Ayub Khan's visit to the United States, it was not fully realized how deep Sino-Indian differences had become; an enlarged conflict or a *rapprochement* were both possible. At this juncture it would not have been expedient to antagonize Pakistan further by continuing to take one measure after another in India's support and against Pakistan's interest. The uncertainty of future developments in the sub-continent called for at least a temporary acceptance of the *status quo*. Time would reveal how deep was the breach in Sino-Indian relations. The Colombo Powers were meanwhile engaged in finding a mutually acceptable solution to a conflict that was more the result of a punitive expedition than an invasion.

This period of marking time was destined to be brief. During Nehru's visit to Washington, in November of the same year, President Kennedy compared him with Abraham Lincoln and Roosevelt. No mention was made of Kashmir in the joint communiqué, which referred to almost all international problems including Berlin, a Nuclear Test Ban Treaty, general and complete disarmament, Laos, and the Congo. That this visit was undertaken shortly before India's attack on Goa in December 1961 is clearly significant. It appears that after his meetings with President Kennedy, Mr. Nehru was in a position to ascertain that the United States would not stand in his way on account of Portuguese membership of NATO. When there was an uproar in the United States over India's seizure of Goa, Dr. Henry Kissinger, President Kennedy's Special Emissary, was sent, in early January 1962, to reassure the Indians that the United States did not intend to take any action against India. On 6 January Dr. Kissinger declared in New Delhi that 'we are not going to spite India because of Goa, in the matter of the

Kashmir dispute when it is raised before Security Council'. On the subject of Pakistan–China relations Dr. Kissinger is reported to have said that if Pakistan were 'stupid enough' to make an alliance with China, 'how long would Asia survive without a strong, independent India?' He also promised the Indians that the United States would support India against invasion from China as it could not permit China to destroy India. As for Portuguese membership of NATO, Dr. Kissinger is reported to have said that he never thought it wise to have included Portugal in the alliance. According to him, Portugal had become a NATO member because at that time America was suffering from a disease called 'Pactitis'. Speaking in Calcutta on 15 January he touched upon Pakistan–China relations and said that he could not believe that Pakistan could make a military alliance with China. He is further reported to have said 'it is inconceivable to me that Pakistan would encourage any aggression against India', and added that it would be inconsistent 'on the part of Pakistan to have military alliance with Communist China as well as the United States though Pakistan has recognized Communist China'. He explained that one reason why he considered an alliance between Pakistan and China to be improper was that Pakistan was allied with the United States and that 'it would not be in the interest of India and Pakistan to bring Communism into the sub-continent to settle their disputes over an issue'. In the same speech he went on to observe that there was no real possibility of Pakistan's entering into an alliance with China to enhance its 'bargaining power'. Explaining the objectives of United States' aid, Dr. Kissinger said that there were two objectives: to stop Communism and to build up a free and prosperous society. In this connection he affirmed that if India used force to 'drive away' China from Indian territory, the United States would be 'most sympathetic' to whatever action the Government of India took against China. In addition to these important declarations made by President Kennedy's Special Emissary, Secretary of State Dean Rusk stated on 7 January that India's action in Goa did not affect American determination to aid India.

These expressions of encouragement to, if not connivance at, India's seizure of Goa, emboldened Indian leaders like the Congress President Sanjiva Reddy to declare on 4 January that

India was 'determined to get Pakistani and Chinese aggression on its soil vacated before long'. He further asserted that 'Cease-fire in Kashmir could not be accepted as a permanent solution of the problem. The whole country is behind the Government in liberating the one-third of Kashmir under Pakistan's illegal occupation.'

The Sino-Indian border conflict of October 1962 removed all doubts as to America's complete support for India. It was now decided to support India even at the risk of alienating Pakistan. This was the opportunity for which the United States had been yearning from the time of Partition—its cherished dream was coming to reality.

The rout of the Indian Army in Ladakh and NEFA evoked immediate reactions in the United States. Without so much as consulting Pakistan, Western allies of the United States were mobilized to render military assistance to India. In the mean-time China unilaterally declared a cease-fire and withdrew its forces; but Mr. Nehru encouraged by the quick and zealous response of the West—and in particular of the United States—declared, in December 1962, that India would continue its military preparations even if the Sino-Indian border dispute was settled. He emphasized that India would make every effort to drive its enemy from the India borders. On 10 December Mr. Averell Harriman observed that the Sino-Indian conflict would endure for a long time; and therefore the United States should continue giving military aid to India. He expressed approval of India's relations with the Soviet Union, which he declared to be in the United States' interest. Nehru said that the Soviet Union had made it clear that it had no objection to India's receiving military and other forms of aid from the United States and Britain.

In the same month, Nehru stressed the historic ties between India and Pakistan and declared that 'confederation remains our ultimate goal, though if we say it they are alarmed and say we want to swallow them up'. At the same time he emphasized that an overall settlement with Pakistan would not be possible while the war with China continued. On 28 December Pakistan and China agreed to sign a boundary treaty. Mr. Galbraith, American Ambassador to India, commented on this news by saying that 'Pakistan should consider American aid as an effort to counter the menace of Communist aggression'.

During these developments President Kennedy and Prime Minister Macmillan met at Nassau, on 18 December, and agreed on an arms aid plan for India amounting to about $120 million, half of which was to be contributed by the British Commonwealth. To buttress the American aid in the military field with political support, Mr. Galbraith informed the Indian Foreign Secretary on 27 December that the United States' aid to fight China was not contingent upon a Kashmir settlement. By giving such an assurance to India before the conclusion of negotiations between India and Pakistan on the Kashmir dispute, the United States wrecked the possibilities of an Indo-Pakistan settlement and so, by its own action, furthered close relations between Pakistan and China. The Indian attitude to the Kashmir negotiations became increasingly negative on account of the repeated assurances given by the United States' Administration that the settlement of the Jammu and Kashmir dispute was not linked with the United States' economic and military support to India. These assurances, coupled with the fact that the Sino-Indian border conflict was over, made India all the more intransigent and brought about a collapse of the Kashmir negotiations. The assurances given by Mr. Galbraith were further supported by Secretary of State Dean Rusk, and reiterated by Mr. Galbraith. Mr. Rusk stated in March 1963 that while the United States' Government believed it 'very important for the security of the entire sub-continent, that India and Pakistan resolve their problems between them . . . I would not in any sense qualify our aid purpose by this word "condition".' Mr. Galbraith restated in late April 1963 that American aid to India was not dependent on a settlement of the Kashmir dispute; and Mr. Nehru also confirmed, in the Lok Sabha on 7 May, that both Mr. Duncan Sandys and Mr. Rusk had assured him that Britain and the United States were not linking the question of military aid to India with a settlement of the Kashmir dispute.

Such an attitude not only jeopardized the settlement of the Jammu and Kashmir dispute, but threatened the territorial integrity of Pakistan. The United States remained unmindful of the dangers to which Pakistan drew attention and believed that Pakistan was exaggerating India's threat to its security.

Not content with extending its influence in India at a cost to Pakistan, the United States showed its disapproval of Pakistan's taking counter-measures to protect its security and territorial integrity. Pakistan's efforts to improve relations with China were misrepresented and attacked in the United States. Double standards were being applied without hesitation. The altered international conditions required the United States to alter its position on alignment and non-alignment, but a corresponding adjustment on the part of Pakistan was not to be tolerated. *The Washington Evening Star* of 25 July 1963 declared:

> Pakistan's fears are understood here, without being respected, and in no sense are they being allowed to dominate American plans for the security of this troubled area. Pakistan may swiftly have reason to repent its decision if it chooses to dilute its alliance with America by co-operation with China.

Yet another pledge to support India was made by Mr. Chester Bowles, the new American Ambassador to India, when, in May 1963, he stated that the United States was 'very anxious to help' India build up her military strength against China. He added 'the only thing to be determined now was the amount of military aid that the Indians can absorb'. On the conclusion of the Indian President's visit to the United States, the joint communiqué issued by President Kennedy and the President of India recorded that: 'their two countries share a mutual defensive concern to thwart the designs of Chinese aggression against the sub-continent. Both the Presidents recognized the vital importance of safeguarding the freedom, independence, and territorial integrity of India for peace and stability not only in Asia but in the world.'[1] On 30 July President Kennedy and Premier Macmillan decided at Birch Grove to provide a United States–Commonwealth umbrella to India in order to 'familiarize' the Indian Air Force with supersonic fighter-bombers; and to draw up schemes to provide further military aid to strengthen her defences against the threat of renewed Chinese Communist attack. Shortly after, the United States was reported to have offered a foreign exchange loan of $80 million to finance an atomic power station at Tarapur near Bombay, designed to be one of the largest in the world.

[1] *Dawn* (Karachi) Editorial, 8 June 1963.

Unconcerned with the many actions prejudicial to the security of Pakistan, the United States continued to express its dissatisfaction over the growing relations between China and Pakistan. In July 1963, commenting on the Air Agreement between Pakistan and China, a Press Officer of the State Department stated that the air link 'could have an adverse effect on efforts to strengthen the security and stability of the sub-continent, which the Chinese Communists want to prevent'. This was followed by General Lucius Clay's remarks, during his testimony before the Senate Foreign Relations Committee, to the effect that he did not believe that the United States can let 'Pakistan dictate our course of action with regard to her neighbour'.

Concluding that the breach between the nations of the sub-continent was final, the United States decided to ignore Pakistan's fears and render long-term military assistance to India. This left Pakistan with the following alternatives:

1. she could liquidate the American bases on her territory and withdraw simultaneously from the bilateral military agreements and from CENTO and SEATO. At the same time she could seek to reach a long-term agreement with the Soviet Union over the supply of military equipment, and make a security pact with the People's Republic of China;

2. she could decide to adopt these measures, but only implement them gradually in response to countermeasures on the part of the United States;

3. while making no overt changes of alignment, she could conclude secret agreements with China;

4. she could retain her existing alignment and make no diplomatic overtures to China and the Soviet Union; or

5. she could play an opportunist role, following no fixed policy, but trimming her sails as the wind blew from one direction or another.

I will say nothing here of the merits and demerits of the various courses open to the Government of Pakistan.

CHAPTER 5

America aids India and ignores Pakistan

The shift in India's foreign policy did not escape the notice of the non-aligned nations of Asia and Africa. Dr. Subandrio, the Foreign Minister of Indonesia, an important non-aligned nation in the community of Asia and Africa, observed on 26 June 1963 that there had been a major shift in his country's foreign policy, because of the 'selfish and heartless attitude of India'. Mr. R. G. Senanayake, a member of the Ceylonese Parliament, gave warning of a potential threat that India might invade Ceylon, and added that 'despite Gandhism, India was doing everything to become an imperialist power by amassing American weapons including warships and submarines'. He went on to declare that 'India's target is Ceylon and not China'. Similar declarations, expressing alarm at India's growing military strength and its abandonment of non-alignment, were made by other prominent Afro-Asian statesmen.

These apprehensions notwithstanding, on 27 July 1963, Mr. Nehru defended India's acceptance of the Western offer of joint air exercises and military equipment by emphasizing that it did not mean any change in the country's foreign policy of neutrality. Later in the year, however, he rejected Western 'air cover' on the ground that foreign bases on Indian soil would compromise India's non-aligned status. In the meantime, it was reported that the Indian request for $100 million emergency military aid was being considered, in addition to the aid promised at Nassau. Moreover, in August 1963, the Aid to India Consortium increased that year's contribution from various countries to India's Third Five Year Plan from $915 million to $1,000 million. The largest additional donor was the United States with an increased contribution of $60 million. In contrast to this, the quantum of aid to Pakistan was not only not being increased, but some of that already pledged by the United States International Agencies was being cut back. The outstanding retraction in the pledged aid was made in the case of the gigantic Tarbela Dam. The delaying tactics over the Steel Mill project, and the suspension of funds for the Dacca Airport, are further examples of that policy. These changes were made despite the World Bank's expressed satisfaction at the utilization of aid in Pakistan and an adverse comment on the misuse of aid funds by India. Congressman Gross pointed out in the House of Representatives that, because the World Bank report was unfavourable to India, the United States' Administration considered it advisable to suppress it.

Feeling assured of continued assistance without any prior conditions on Kashmir, Mr. Nehru declared in the Lok Sabha on 13 August 1963 that ' "the concessions" which we offered to Pakistan [for a settlement of the Kashmir dispute] are no longer open and they must be treated as withdrawn'. Commenting on Mr. Nehru's *volte face*, *The Washington Post* said that:

Nehru speaks from his own bitter experience of personal failure in the thirty-year search for a Hindu-Muslim peace prior to partition when he argues that the overall tenor of Indo-Pakistan relations might well remain essentially the same after the Kashmir settlement. Pakistan would still be reliving the trauma of partition. India would still be the great power of the region and would be more determined than ever after relinquishing Kashmir to exact Pakistan's acknowledgement of the intrinsic power relationship between the two countries.

As Pakistan's relations with the United States slipped from one crisis to another, President Kennedy felt it necessary to touch upon the complexity of the United States' relations with India and Pakistan, saying in a press statement on 12 September 1963:

The fact, of course, is we want to sustain India, which may be attacked this fall by China. So we do not want India to be helpless as a half billion people. . . . Of course, if that country becomes fragmented and defeated, of course, that would be a most destructive blow to the balance of power.

On the other hand, everything we give to India adversely affects the balance of power with Pakistan, which is a much smaller country. So we are dealing with a very, very complicated problem, because the hostility between them is so deep.

George Ball's trip was an attempt to lessen that. I think we are going to deal with a very unsatisfactory situation in that area.[1]

[1] *Dawn* (Karachi), 14 September 1963.

Overlooking the delicate balance of power in the sub-continent, the United States' Government did not wait to consult Pakistan before rendering large-scale military assistance to India in the aftermath of its autumn 1962 border conflict with China; this despite President Kennedy's earlier undertaking to President Ayub Khan that Pakistan would be so consulted. At first the United States' Government made the grant of military assistance to India conditional on the settlement of the Jammu and Kashmir dispute, but when Mr. Nehru refused to relent, the condition was withdrawn. The Pakistan Government's repeated apprehension that the growth of India's military machine would increase the threat to Pakistan's security, and contribute to greater tensions between India and China, proved to be of no avail. The salient steps taken during President Kennedy's time to strengthen India's defences were as follows:

1. At Nassau, on 18–21 December 1962, after the cease-fire on the Indo-China border had taken place, the United States and Britain decided to continue to supply India on an emergency basis with up to $120,000,000 worth of military aid. The programme included a variety of military equipment but its central feature was the arming of six Indian Divisions for mountain warfare.
2. As a result of the Nassau decision, a United States–Britain–Canadian Air Mission visited India to examine what would be India's air needs should China attack again.
3. Another US Mission went to India to assess the question of expanding India's capacity for production of arms.
4. On 30 June 1963, at Birch Grove, the United States and Britain decided on a further substantial programme of military aid to India, over and above that amount agreed to at Nassau. This enabled India to decide to raise her standing army from 11 to 22 divisions as rapidly as possible and to expand substantially her air force and navy.[1]

After the assassination of President Kennedy in November 1963, his successor, President Johnson, continued on the same path. On 27 December of that year *Time* magazine reported that Nehru had now agreed to accept the Western air defence umbrella and the United States' Seventh Fleet in the Indian Ocean, but, in return, he had asked for $1·5 billion military

[1] *Dawn* (Karachi), 18 October 1963.

assistance to secure his concurrence. In March 1964 the United States' Defence Secretary, Mr. Robert McNamara, repeated the American determination to continue the programme of military support to India. He stated that the United States planned to continue the 'modernization of a number of Mountain Divisions of the Indian Army and would also provide certain other "assistance" '. He acknowledged that military assistance to India had 'deeply troubled' Pakistan but felt that 'it is important to the entire free world, including Pakistan, that India be able to defend itself against Communist Chinese aggression'. The Defence Secretary forcefully pleaded for continued support to Iran, Pakistan, and India, and described these nations as being on the 'front line of the free world defence against Communist encroachment in the near East and South Asia'. So it was made clear that the United States now considered India to be virtually a member of an unwritten alliance against Communism and entitled to rights and privileges at least equal to those of SEATO and CENTO members; but with the all-important difference that India would be permitted to maintain its veneer of non-alignment and be free from awkward and perilous obligations which reciprocally bound other aligned nations.

On 1 March 1964 Mr. George Ball, the United States' Under-Secretary of State, warned Pakistan that 'we very much hope President Ayub will not carry relations with Red China to a point where it impairs a relationship which we have and an alliance which we have'. He added that 'what it [Pakistan's relations with China] reflects in terms of an attitude is something about which we are very much concerned. We watch this very carefully.' And he went on to say:

Pakistan . . . is very clear about her enemy being the Soviet Union and about the fact that she is a member of an alliance which is directed against Communist aggression, and I am sure that if there were any move by Red China against Pakistan, then Pakistan would respond with military defence. Her discussions with Red China up to this point have not suggested otherwise, but we are watching this relationship with great attention.

In April 1964 Phillips Talbot, Assistant Secretary of State for Near East and South Asian Affairs, told the United States House of Representatives Foreign Affairs Committee:

At the same time, Pakistan has moved to take advantage of

Communist overtures, designed to isolate India, by concluding trade, boundary, and civil air agreements with Red China and by expanding cultural exchanges.

We have made clear our concern and our belief that even if marginal benefits may accrue to Pakistan from these measures, the political effect is to give advantage to an enemy against which we are formally allied.

Here, as elsewhere, we must seek to accomplish our objective without infringing upon the sovereign rights of another Government. We continue to believe that our national interests and those of Pakistan coincide and that this is recognized by Pakistan as well.[1]

Parallel with the mounting criticism of Pakistan, American support for India continued to grow. At this juncture, not perhaps fortuitously, the idea of confederation, originally aired by Nehru, was picked up by *The New York Times* and *The Washington Post*. Both these influential newspapers advocated confederation between India and Pakistan, linked by a joint defence over Kashmir. Many other influential sources—both official and unofficial—expressed similar views. Unofficial emissaries made frequent visits to the sub-continent to assess the prospects of Indo-Pakistan confederation. During this time, in testimonies before Congress, United States' officials voiced the opinion that containment of China in south-east Asia was more important than the settlement of the Kashmir dispute. Phillips Talbot told the Foreign Affairs Committee that, as far as the United States' aid programmes went, the main American concern was:

to balance the various aspects of our relationship in South Asia. If Kashmir were the most important thing in the world to the United States, then I would think that it would be our duty to say, no more aid to either country until the Kashmir dispute is settled. If, on the other hand, in the sub-continent it is more important to limit the opportunity of the Communist powers to move in, to limit potential disintegration and chaos in those two countries so that they can develop viability and they can be effective nations of the world, then we should take what measures we can to help them constructively and in our diplomatic efforts, try very hard to help them soften these bone-deep cultural, religious, social, economic, and political disputes.

[1] *Dawn* (Karachi), 11 April 1964.

Mr. William S. Gaud, Deputy Administrator of Aid, was more outspoken when he told the House Committee that 'while Kashmir is an important issue, it is not an essential issue in that part of the world as far as we are concerned'. On 18 June 1964 Mr. Dean Rusk reaffirmed the importance of the United States remaining 'steadfast in its support to Indian economic development and defence efforts during the coming year'. In his statement the Secretary of State mentioned some 'key problem areas where United States' aid is a factor'. They included South Vietnam, India, Brazil, Africa, and Cyprus. No mention was made of Pakistan.

The idea of 'a coalition of Asian powers with India as its main force to counter-balance China's power' was expressed again in September 1964, when Senator Hubert Humphrey supported it during his election campaign for the vice-presidency. According to his view, the United States was to decide the 'long range political future of Asia' and was to make India 'strong enough to exercise leadership in the area'. When the People's Republic of China detonated its first atomic bomb in late 1964, Mr. Chester Bowles reassured India that 'a closer military alliance with United States could bring the entire nuclear power of the Seventh Fleet into frontier struggle on the side of India, and India would have not only the atomic bombs, but the much more devastating hydrogen bombs at her disposal in the Fleet arsenal of weapons'. In February 1965 Mr. McNamara, accusing China of 'trying to drive a wedge between Pakistan and the United States', saw 'a very real need for India to improve the quantity of its defence against the Chinese Communist threat'. He believed that 'it is in our interest to assist them'.

As a mark of its disapproval of Pakistan's growing relations with China, the United States' Government postponed the Consortium meeting of aid to Pakistan in July 1965 by two months on the excuse that congressional authorization had not yet been given, and that, pending appropriation by Congress, the United States was not in a position to pledge financial aid for the first year of Pakistan's Third Five Year Plan. This decision was taken by the United States' Government without consulting other Consortium countries. In communicating the postponement from July to September 1965, the American

Ambassador to Pakistan gave President Ayub Khan a message from President Johnson which stated that, if Pakistan so wished, she could discuss certain other problems in this period. By contrast, the aid to India was sanctioned a little earlier by the Aid to India Consortium, and before congressional authorization was obtained. The Consortium meeting was abruptly postponed to exert undisguised pressure on Pakistan. Shortly after conveying President Johnson's message to President Ayub Khan, the American Ambassador called on me and spelt out the 'matters' requiring discussion before the Consortium could meet to consider Pakistan's economic needs. These matters covered the whole range of Pakistan's relations with the Peoples' Republic of China, with President Soekarno's regime, and Vietnam.

The United States' Government's commitment to come to Pakistan's assistance in the event of India misusing its aid is evident beyond doubt. In addition to the terms of SEATO and CENTO and those of the bilateral defence agreements, the former United States' Ambassador in Pakistan, Mr. Walter P. McConnaughy, stated in Hyderabad, on 31 October 1962, that the United States would take every precaution that the 'assistance' provided to India to help her fight the Chinese would not be used against Pakistan. In November 1962 the United States gave a guarantee that she would come to the direct assistance of Pakistan in the case of aggression from outside, including India. Ambassador McConnaughy again declared in a Press Conference in Karachi, on 9 November 1962, that 'The United States in turn has assured the Pakistan Government officially that if this assistance to India should be misused and misdirected against another country in aggression, the United States would undertake immediately, in accordance with constitutional authority, appropriate action both within and without the United Nations to thwart such aggression by India'. This statement was a reiteration of the one made by the State Department on the previous day. Speaking on the same subject, on 20 November 1962, President Kennedy told a Press Conference:

In providing military assistance to India, we are mindful of our alliance with Pakistan. All of our aid to India is for the purpose of defeating Chinese Communist subversion. Chinese incursions into the sub-continent are a threat to Pakistan as well as India, and both have a common interest in opposing it. We have urged this point in both Governments. Our help to India in no way diminishes or qualifies our commitment to Pakistan and we have made this clear to both Governments as well.[1]

At the end of the statement he touched on the point mentioned in the joint communiqué issued in Washington on 13 July 1961, during President Ayub Khan's visit to the United States. That had stated:

The two Presidents re-affirmed the solemn purpose of the bilateral agreements signed by the two Governments on March 5th, 1959, which declared among other things that 'the Government of the United States of America regards as vital to its national interest and to world peace the preservation of the independence and integrity of Pakistan'.[2]

Recapitulating all previous assurances, Ambassador McConnaughy said that 'in addition to these public statements of American policy, direct assurances of a similar nature have been given to the Government of Pakistan. The record is clear. The policy of the United States in regard to the independence and defence of Pakistan remains unchanged.' On 17 September 1963 Mr. Phillips Talbot gave the following confirmation of American assurances:

I think that the leaders of the Government of Pakistan understand our concern for the security of Pakistan, just as the leaders of India understand our concern for the security of India. And both, I believe, recognize that in what we regard as the highly unlikely event that either country should attack the other, there would be an American response.[3]

Addressing the House of Representatives Foreign Affairs Committee on 25 March 1964, Mr. McNamara reiterated that the United States had taken 'great pains to assure Pakistan that our aid to India will not be at the expense of Pakistan security to which we are committed under our Mutual Defence Arrangements'.

[1] *Dawn* (Karachi), 3 August 1963.
[2] ibid.
[3] ibid., 19 September 1963.

The gradual whittling down of both economic and military assistance to Pakistan since 1962, and the progressive increase in military and economic assistance to India, were beginning to exercise deleterious political influences, besides widening the imbalance between India and Pakistan. In spite of the assurances given to Pakistan, a growing sense of uneasiness spread through the country as the balance tilted each day more in India's favour. The Indian attitude towards Pakistan was becoming more defiant. This was chiefly demonstrated in Kashmir, the focal point of the conflict. India had not taken any drastic measures to integrate Jammu and Kashmir in the Indian Union until the United States decided to provide her with military assistance. Then in late 1963, without any justification, India marched her troops into the village of Chaknot in Azad Kashmir. This and other provocative demonstrations of chauvinism were repeated with greater bravado as the position of the United States became clearer. Almost a year after the occupation of Chaknot, in October 1964, Prime Minister Shastri declared as a matter of set policy the integration of the occupied territory of Jammu and Kashmir into India. When Pakistan lodged a protest with the United States, Mr. Harriman merely expressed his 'shock and surprise' and promised to convey American 'anxieties' about it to New Delhi. That India's bold adventures in Kashmir were the outcome of United States' military, economic, and political support did not escape the attention of many well-informed political observers, such as Bertrand Russell who said:

In Kashmir, India has refused to allow a plebiscite for many years, despite United Nations resolutions. One hundred thousand Indian troops have suppressed Kashmiri autonomy. Despite all this for seventeen years Mr. Nehru held back from invoking the two Articles of the Indian Constitution which would integrate Kashmir by decree. We must ask why Premier Shastri invoked those two Articles, arrested Shaikh Abdullah and thereby effectively closed the door to peaceful redress of the Kashmiris' grievances. The answer to this question suggests the cause of the outbreak of this war. . . . The official integration of Kashmir made the uprising in the valley inevitable and the participation in the uprising of Kashmiris from Pakistan had to be expected.[1]

[1] *Dawn* (Karachi), 29 April 1965.

Prime Minister Shastri initiated a policy towards the sub-jugated State which even Nehru dared not adopt. It was rapidly integrated, the relevant articles of the Indian Constitution en-suring autonomy for Kashmir were abrogated, the Civil Service in the disputed territory was 'Indianized', political leaders from Shaikh Abdullah down were put behind bars, popular agitation over the Hazrat Bal Shrine incident was ruthlessly suppressed, and the cease-fire line invoked as an excuse to eject Muslims from the border regions into Pakistan and replace them by militant Sikh and Dogra populations. Except for the arrest of leaders, none of these actions had been taken in all the years of Nehru's Prime Ministership. In this way the situation was deliberately brought to a head.

As a follow-up, and to test Pakistan's resolve, India em-barked on military operations in the Rann of Kutch in April 1965. An offensive probe was put into operation to ascertain Pakistan's political and military responses and to determine the extent to which she was prepared to defend her frontiers. Although the battle went badly for the Indian forces, and Pakistan was in a position to inflict a humiliating defeat on them, the restraint exercised in not pressing these military advantages encouraged the Indians to believe that Pakistan would refrain from military action in retaliation to India's plans to annex Jammu and Kashmir. At the same time, rea-lizing that there would come an end to Pakistan's restraint and that she would not indefinitely endure one serious provocation after another, India took the precaution of simultaneously attacking Lahore to foreclose the Kashmir issue by the use of force. On the other hand, if Pakistan had taken advantage of its military successes in the Rann of Kutch and completed the operations in that sector by annihilating a complete Indian division and occupied Karim Shahi, to which it had a right, India would have regained her senses and not precipitated another conflict only five months later.

When, on 6 September 1965, India launched her attack on Pakistan, all but two or three of the nations of the world ex-pressed shock and disapproval. The British Prime Minister deplored the Indian crossing of the cease-fire line; President Nasser made it plain to Krishna Menon that the attack on Lahore was a gross violation of international frontiers; the

People's Republic of China gave an ultimatum to India to end her aggression or be prepared for Chinese intervention; and Iran, Turkey, and Indonesia gave moral and material support to Pakistan. At Casablanca, all the Arab states condemned the attack on Pakistan and, in the United Nations, the overwhelming majority of countries from Latin America, Africa, and Asia were severely critical of India's aggression. There was widespread sympathy for Pakistan in Western and Eastern Europe. The United States showed great concern at the outbreak of hostilities, but, instead of implementing its many assurances by coming to the assistance of its attacked ally Pakistan, the United States' Government confined its energies and influence to bringing about a cease-fire. With this end in view an embargo was imposed on both countries, by which the United States chose to equate the aggressor with the victim of aggression. While Pakistan received its military supplies only from the United States, India received its armaments from the Soviet Union and many other countries and manufactured locally most of the light equipment and ammunition; so the embargo, in actual fact, operated exclusively to Pakistan's disadvantage.

Much more will be written about the war and of other nations' attitudes to it, but until further information can be made available, it is enough to say that great disappointment was felt in Pakistan at the American attitude. Had the United States not changed its policies, India would not have embarked on her bold adventure in a hurry. She would not have dared to attack Pakistan if there was the fear that the United States would fulfil her treaty obligations and other commitments to Pakistan. If the military balance had not been altered, India would not have been in a position to mount the attack. The six mountain divisions which were formed and equipped by the United States for the purpose of facing the Chinese were turned against Pakistan in Kashmir. Pakistan, a member of CENTO and SEATO, a client of long standing, and a victim of aggression by a country five times its size, found its principal ally more anxious to search for a cease-fire than to come to its rescue. The American point of view has, of course, to be considered. President Ayub Khan went to meet President Johnson in Washington in December 1965, hoping that from their dialogue would emerge a better understanding of each other's position. A number of steps were taken by Pakistan as a measure of her penance and to honour the new understanding reached in Washington. The impression began to gain currency that slowly, one by one, the shards of the precious urn of special relations, which had been shattered in the aftermath of the 1965 war, were being picked up and pieced together. Action was taken in every direction to reduce what the journalists called 'irritants'.

The United States' decision to terminate military assistance to Pakistan thus came as a shock to those who believed that the serene days of the special relationship were returning. Global Powers do not act in pique; nor do they lose sight of their objectives under pressure of exigencies. On occasions, they may seek time to remove an impediment or misunderstanding, but that is only the exterior manifestation of a diplomacy under which lie deep motivations. As it is claimed that the decision to stop military assistance was intended to bring about Indo-Pakistani co-operation, it is necessary to examine what is meant by this 'co-operation' and why so much emphasis is being placed on this word.

Constitutional terms like 'confederation' and 'condominium' are outdated. Moreover, in the sub-continent they are charged with historical prejudices of a kind that make people distrust their use. Once a meeting of minds has taken place and a common purpose evolved, formulas can always be found to translate co-operation into constitutional language. What is important is not the outward expression but the actual substance of co-operation. There are countries whose federal or confederate structure is of no help in producing harmonious relations between the component units. One might take Nigeria as an example of a country where inner discords between the federative units have not ceased to create trouble. On the other hand, though Canada and the United States are linked by no constitutional arrangement, their manner of co-operation transcends formal arrangements.

According to the American view, a meeting of minds is necessary before a more formal and defined association can be considered. As a first step in this direction, tensions must be eased and disputes frozen. With their armies no more facing each other, two countries can look for common goals, instead of wasting effort in a hunt for outmoded legal arrangements which only accentuate suspicions and excite prejudices. If India and Pakistan were to set aside their differences, that, in itself, would be a negative form of co-operation. They could then be brought together to face the supposed common enemy, Communist China. From the American point of view, once the direction of relations changes, the task of achieving a large area of co-operation is considerably simplified, even to the extent of leading to a future constitutional link. To this end, as an essential prerequisite, every endeavour was being made to bring about Indo-Pakistani co-operation.

CHAPTER 6

American Policy to bring Pakistan under Indian Hegemony

Force enters when diplomacy is exhausted. If all attempts to bring about co-operation between India and Pakistan fail, it would be imprudent to rule out coercive measures. This does not necessarily mean that the United States, whose objectives are not quite identical with those of India, would, in desperation, create conditions that would enable India to dismember or destroy Pakistan. However, if the lessons of September 1965 are not forgotten, it would be rash to discount this possibility altogether in the calculations of Pakistan's foreign and defence policies.

The history of Pakistan–United States relations has been out-lined in the preceding chapters to clarify the implications of present developments. It is high time that, after two decades of independence, we learned to approach events more systematic-ally and to put an end to the age-old habit of impetuous and arbitrary *ad hoc* responses.

On the face of it, the decision of 12 April 1967 was taken to restrain the arms race between India and Pakistan and prevent another war. It was also supposedly intended to divert defence expenditures to agricultural and industrial development. In the first place, however, an arms *balance* between India and Pakistan is likely to reduce the risk of war. This has been borne out by our experience of the last twenty years. Outside the sub-continent, and on a much larger scale, there is the example of the existing military balance between the Soviet Union and the United States, which has led not to war but to a *détente*. The temptation to wage war normally arises when there is a military imbalance. After a period of time, the effect of the United States' decision will lead to a situation in which India would be in a strong position to strike at Pakistan. It does not, therefore, necessarily follow that an arms race between India and Pakistan would, *ipso facto*, lead to war. It has been contended that an arms balance can also be obtained by a reduction of armed forces. How that is both dangerous and impracticable will be demonstrated later. Only vigilance and preparedness are likely to prevent war, and neither a bilateral reduction of armed forces nor an advantage in India's favour will prevent catastrophe. Even more obvious is the fallacy that the United States' decision was taken in order to prevent war between India and Pakistan. Independent of an arms race, India and Pakistan have been permanently in a state of either enmity or acute confrontation; only the degree of tension has varied. Their relations have never been normal and are not capable of becoming normal without the settlement of fundamental disputes that have smouldered since Partition. The United States has always been aware of this inflammable situation, but nevertheless concluded Mutual Defence Agreements with Pakistan and welcomed Pakistan's membership of SEATO and CENTO. Indeed, it went to the extent of giving assurances to Pakistan that it would assist Pakistan in the event of aggression from India. From the time of Independence, both India and Pakistan began to strengthen their armed forces and the United States has been the principal contributor to this arms race. It remained the most important source of military supplies at the height of our tensions. In 1954, after defence agreements were concluded, the United States began to supply military equipment to Pakistan, much to the anger of India. Following the Sino-Indian conflict in 1962, the United States gave military assistance to India and ignored Pakistan's protests that this would prompt Indian aggression. Commenting on the traffic in military weapons in the Middle East after the 1967 conflict, James Reston made a pertinent observation:

The Administration is simultaneously making speeches against the dumping of modern and obsolete arms on all kinds of countries and steadily making shipments of more and more arms. In fact, the United States government is now sending more weapons to more countries than any other nation in the world.

The facts are startling: from 1949 to June 1966, the United States government alone (not counting the private arms salesmen) sold $16·1 billion in military arms to other countries and gave away a total of $30·2 billion. This $46·3 billion amounts, over the same period, to $4 billion more than all the economic grants and loans provided to other countries by the United States since the middle of 1948, including the spectacularly successful Marshall Plan.[1]

The United States cannot justifiably withhold arms on the grounds that it would lead to an arms race between India and Pakistan; nor can it be seriously contended that the decision to stop military assistance to Pakistan is influenced either by the desire to prevent war or an arms race leading to war. Turkey and Greece receive massive arms assistance from the United States, and more than once have been on the brink of war over Cyprus; yet the United States has not suspended its military assistance to either of them. This differentiation has been made because the centre of the cold war has shifted from Europe to Asia, where the struggle against Communism has, in effect, now come to mean the struggle against the People's Republic of China.

It cannot be seriously contended either that military assistance has been stopped to divert defence expenditure for economic development, with the pious purpose of making India and Pakistan more prosperous. From the very beginning, India and Pakistan have been spending a large part of their resources on defence and yet, for many years, the United States continued to supply arms to both countries without political or economic preconditions. India and Pakistan have not suddenly become poor. Famine and poverty are not new phenomena to arouse the conscience of the United States into curtailing defence expenditures so that the money can be spent elsewhere. If the American Government had actually felt that the economic welfare of Pakistan took precedence over its territorial integrity, it would not have given massive military assistance for so long to two poor countries, historical adversaries of one another. Since the end of the Second World War nations everywhere have seen that economic vulnerability opens the doors to foreign interference. If India and Pakistan had been economically self-sufficient, it is doubtful if they would have had a dominant foreign presence on their soil. Thus, the factors that attract foreign intervention cannot be repugnant to Powers seeking to enlarge their influence in the affairs of other states. It would be

[1] *International Herald Tribune*, 22–23 July 1967, p. 4.

an elementary contradiction to remove maladies which invite interference and are responsible for the spread of influence.

What then has caused this major change in the historical position of the United States? There is no significant new internal factor in the sub-continent to account for it. India and Pakistan were at war over their unresolved disputes in 1948, years before the United States stepped in with military assistance. The arms race between them began before the United States gave it impetus; and there was poverty in both countries much before the United States sought to diversify their defence expenditures to eradicate economic ills. All the old conditions remain unaltered. New factors, however, have appeared outside the sub-continent, and their emergence has exaggerated the existing problems of the sub-continent and given them a new sense of urgency. These external factors, which have caused a general reappraisal in Washington, are the precarious state of the Vietnam war and the growing power of China in Asia. This situation has to be controlled, and it cannot be done effectively without the co-operation of India and Pakistan.

These factors were not present in 1954 and they had not assumed their present proportions in 1962; but recent developments have necessitated many decisions, including the one announced on 12 April 1967. It is not true that the United States wants to retire from the sub-continent in disgust. No country has tried harder to extend its influence in the two countries, yet the United States has taken a decision which, on the surface, gives an impression of withdrawal from the most sensitive area of contact between Great Powers and under-developed countries. Can it be argued that the United States considers the situation to be so hopeless that any further investment would be unproductive? Is it conceivable that the greatest Power on earth would suddenly write off six hundred million people and a strategically important sub-continent? Such an abdication is out of the question, especially at a time when America has made it abundantly clear that it will leave no void to Communism. It remains America's primary objective to increase its influence in the sub-continent and to make this region a bastion of the 'free world' in Asia. Only eight days before the State Department announced its decision to stop military assistance to India and Pakistan, the United States'

Secretary of State, Mr. Dean Rusk, appealed to Pakistan and India 'to find some way to achieve genuine co-operation in the sub-continent', and went on to inform the House of Representatives Foreign Affairs Committee that 'such co-operation would constitute a formidable bulwark of the free world strength'.

An American President not so long ago observed that it would not be possible to hold Asia if the sub-continent were lost to Communism. If the United States is prepared to risk world conflagration in order to hold the line against Communism in Vietnam, is it likely to walk out of the sub-continent and so forsake its position in Asia for all time? Let it be clearly understood that the announcement to terminate military assistance does not herald a retreat. On the contrary, it is an overt demonstration of strength and an ultimatum to the countries involved. In the past, the United States took the position that it was not able to influence India and Pakistan to arrive at a settlement of their disputes, maintaining that its aid was not given to coerce either country. As its influence was insufficient to bring them to terms on the basis of its own interests, it desisted from exercising its coercive power. Its strong presence in one country and its relatively weak presence in the other fell short of the requirement for punitive action. With the lapse of time, however, the United States has deeply penetrated both and now feels that its influence is, for the first time, of such magnitude that it can take the risk of exercising simultaneous pressure on both of them to bring them together.

Since the Sino-Indian conflict of 1962 and the decline in India's prestige, the United States has gradually assumed a position of commanding influence in that country. India would face unbearable hardships without the ten million tons of food which the United States supplies to it annually, and which the United States alone can provide. Even if past credits and servicing of debts are set aside, and even if the internal chaos in India is discounted, its present dependence on the United States, and Pakistan's established dependence, are sufficient factors for the United States to conclude that such an advantageous position is not likely to endure for ever. Assistance to both countries has never been higher; consequently, their dependence has never been greater; and the United States

urgently needs sub-continental adjustments. On every consideration, global and regional, long-term and immediate, this is the
opportune moment to bring Pakistan and India finally together for the attainment of the United States' objectives in
Asia and elsewhere. Now is the time to cash the dividends from
two decades of colossal investment.

The Soviet Union also wants a settlement of Indo-Pakistani
disputes, but for different reasons. Up to a point the interests
of the two Global Powers are similar. The announcement made
in Washington on 12 April 1967 states that the Soviet Union,
among other nations, was consulted and informed of the United
States' decision to stop military assistance to India and Pakistan.
If the two Global Powers are acting in concert to force a settlement between India and Pakistan, it would mean that Pakistan
would have to make greater sacrifices and pursue a bolder
policy of friendship with the People's Republic of China. If,
however, the Soviet Union is not acting in conformity with the
United States and will not co-operate in forcing a settlement by
the use of collective aid levers, it would be less difficult for
Pakistan to retain its neutrality.

The Soviet Union seeks peace between India and Pakistan
to contain the influence of the United States and China. The
United States seeks peace between the two countries to prevent
the spread of Soviet influence in the sub-continent and to make
India and Pakistan jointly face China. This is the important
difference and it would have been conclusive, if Sino-Soviet
differences had not become so deep. The Soviet Union is unlikely to press Pakistan with the same degree of intensity as the
United States to take second place to India and openly to
assume a belligerent attitude towards China. The United States,
on the other hand, would like Pakistan to co-operate with
India, thus completing the encirclement of China from this
end of Asia. The sub-continent is the one gap yet to be filled.
Time alone will show to what extent the Soviet Union will
co-operate with the United States to meet a part of their common objective. The Soviet Union's position might remain close
to that of the United States for some time, but it is doubtful if
the proximity of interest is likely to endure indefinitely. The
time has surely come for the Soviet Union to redefine its global
role and remove the doubts occasioned by its being pushed into

one compromise after another by the United States. In any event, Pakistan is capable of exercising considerable manœuvrability to negotiate a more favourable future relationship with the Soviet Union. But if time and opportunity are allowed to slip, the belated initiatives will lose meaning, which would be a great tragedy for Pakistan's diplomacy.

The United States' position is fairly clear. What it is after is in its highest global interest and to that extent understandable. The fact that Pakistan has to pay a high price is relevant only to the people of Pakistan. It would be better to face the ordeal dispassionately rather than with a torrent of protest, which subsides without any corresponding benefit to the national cause. This is not the first crisis in Pakistan's relations with the United States. The pattern has been fairly evident for quite some time. Each successive action the United States has taken has been for the attainment of fixed objectives. Each crisis has been followed by voluble press comments and a spate of statements, which are afterwards relegated to the archives. This strategy could be described as a 'Please—Punch' approach, a method to confuse the leadership of Pakistan and weaken the resolve of its people against an overall compromise.

An action is taken to move Pakistan towards global alignment, which occasions loud but ineffectual protests. Then an economic carrot is dangled in front of the Pakistan Government to persuade its official spokesmen to return to their desks. The inducement has taken many forms: the supply of food under PL-480, on conditions varying with the requirements of United States' diplomacy; project and commodity aid, determined separately and collectively in Consortium meetings held twice a year by the World Bank; project aid outside the consortium, as in support of the Indus Basin Treaty and salinity and waterlogging projects; support for the Pakistani rupee; and the utilization of counterpart funds for rural development and other similar projects. Again, after a decent lapse of time, comes another punch prompting protests which are soothed by further economic palliatives; and so the caravan moves towards its destination. This pattern of action began in November 1959, when there was a border skirmish between India and China on the heights of the Ladakh plateau. The present position is simply the inevitable outcome of changed conditions. New situations have brought about a change in the United States' objectives in the sub-continent and, hence, Pakistan has had to watch one crisis follow another.

With the change of the United States' attitude, neutrality and non-alignment, once denounced by Dulles as immoral, began to gain respectability. The world was reminded of India's importance, of the vastness of her territory, and the significance of her large population. There were pressing reasons why she should be made a show-piece of democracy in Asia. In 1961 disproportionate economic assistance was allocated to non-aligned India in preference to aligned Pakistan, but Pakistan did not repair the damage by approaching the Soviet Union and China. In those days the Russian response might have been favourable, because the Sino-Soviet differences had not erupted into the open and the *détente* between the Soviet Union and the United States had not crystallized. Pakistan, however, reacted with platitudinous paper propaganda, soon to be silenced by the servile acceptance of some economic aid. The next painful punch came during the Sino-Indian border clash of 1962, when the United States seized the opportunity to pour in massive military assistance to India in contravention of its commitments to Pakistan. Subsequently, a long-term military assistance commitment was made in 1964 to non-aligned, neutral India to the peril of aligned Pakistan, in violation of a prior commitment. In short, the sub-continent's frantic arms race was introduced and encouraged by the United States.

Then came the conflict between India and Pakistan in 1965. If this was not a sufficient lesson for us, the present crisis in Pakistan–United States relations is not likely to be more educative. China, the country against which SEATO was constructed, demonstrated its sympathy and support for Pakistan, a member of that alliance. The tragedy of Pakistan's foreign policy has its ironic scenes. With its alliance torn to shreds, the country was compelled to explore new avenues to safeguard its national security and territorial integrity. Could that be done by trying to re-establish a special relationship with the United States on a subjective basis, as was attempted in December 1965? Objective considerations have hitherto frustrated every endeavour directed towards such a tenuous *rapprochement*. The search for national security has to be made in a different manner and in other directions. The United States' attitude will continue to stiffen until Pakistan agrees to its terms or draws a line and says 'thus far and no further'. The latest example of the United States' 'Please—Punch' strategy is the commitment on Tarbela made to placate Pakistan. The inevitable punch followed on 12 April 1967, when the stoppage of military assistance was announced. Whether Pakistan is in a position to alter the present course of its relations with the United States can only be known when resistance is offered. Pakistan's national interests must be safeguarded, even at the expense of displeasing the United States. This does not mean that Pakistan has physically to confront the power of the United States, but only that we have to make it resolutely clear by diplomatic, political, and economic means that we will never permit the gradual erosion of our national interests. Such a stand would require internal adjustments and sacrifices but not, necessarily, lasting tension with the United States. One passing crisis is preferable to a succession of crises punctuated by periodical respites, leading to an ineluctable emergency, when it might be beyond Pakistan's means to redeem its position.

Pressure is an impolite word. It is bad manners to employ it in the language of diplomacy, which is not to say that nations have not exercised pressure in the past. In the age of physical domination, coercion was exercised in a crude fashion. In our neo-colonial times, methods of coercion are more refined, as India and Pakistan have not been alone in discovering. Some countries have been able to resist submission to the hegemony of Global Powers, others have not. We in Pakistan, however, are concerned with our own situation. Our dependence on the United States in the military field has been total and not inconsiderable in economic and food requirements. The implementation of the Indus Basin Treaty has also to be taken into account. The intensity of pressure on Pakistan will be much greater than on India for the simple reason that the demand on Pakistan is of a much higher order. The pressures will increase until resistance is offered or until we throw up our hands in submission. If we run, we shall have to keep running until we collapse. The pressures on India will also grow, but they will be less severe, as has already been demonstrated by the stoppage of military assistance, a decision entirely unfavourable to

G

Pakistan. Thus, intensive pressure on Pakistan and moderate pressure on India will be applied simultaneously; and now that the war in the Middle East has ended in victory for America's ally, the United States will press the more heavily on India and Pakistan. After a brief respite, when the political situation in the Middle East gets clearer and the General Assembly files one more resolution, the United States will turn its full attention to the sub-continent for the achievement of its global aims.

In 1958 the United States was not in a position to coerce India, but that situation has changed. Advantage has been taken of the general disarray in India, of the appalling famine conditions, to make the first inroads. As in the case of Pakistan, pressure was initially applied in the economic and financial spheres. This was done to test India's responses; to see if, like Pakistan, she would gradually succumb to one pressure after another, leading to the final show of strength. As in the case of Pakistan, it all started in the spirit of the good Samaritan. Advice was proffered on fiscal policies leading to the devaluation of the Indian rupee. Elated by this success, the United States moved forward to interfere in the industrial and agricultural policies of India. The Indian Government was advised to grant concessions to private entrepreneurs in order to strengthen the fabric of free enterprise. The Indian Government, harassed by mounting difficulties and the spectre of famine, capitulated. These results apparently encouraged the United States to come out into the open by terminating military assistance to both countries with the object of compelling them to submit to a broader agreement. After two decades of painstaking effort, circumstances conspired to place the United States in a commanding position in India and Pakistan. It has been a notable triumph of twenty years of diplomatic tenacity. The United States has every reason to feel satisfied with the hold it exercises over the six hundred million people of the sub-continent, where at the end of the Second World War it had no influence. After so much patient labour the time has come to reap the harvest and, on 12 April 1967, Washington made a demand for the repayment of the first instalment of its astronomical investments.

Far from heralding a withdrawal from the sub-continent, the United States' decision must be construed as a forward thrust, a calculated step to dictate terms to India and Pakistan. The history of our sub-continent is rich in examples of interference by European Powers ever since the English and the French first landed on the coast and acquired settlement rights in certain places. Aided by knowledge of that history, the United States has repeated the pattern of imperial influence. Clive's Diwani has a counterpart in the economic concessions and military facilities that have been given to the Americans. The establishment of settlements at Calcutta, Madras, Pondicherry, and other places from which the European Powers enlarged their influence, has its modern equivalent. It might be said that the extension of America's influence in our sub-continent is rather different from the concessions given to the European trading communities, and there are indeed differences; but why should one see less danger in today's foreign military base than in the peaceful trading stations of the past? Those peaceful trading stations turned out to be bridgeheads for conquest. In what way are military bases any less dangerous? Every military concession accorded by an Asian country is a source of danger to it. The perils are so grave that France liquidated foreign bases on her territory by serving notice on NATO. India and Pakistan have already given the equivalent of the Diwani of Bengal, bestowed by the Mughal Emperor on Clive, in order to obtain foreign economic and military assistance. It seems that neither country has learnt the lesson from that part of our inglorious past that brought about the subjugation of our people for almost two hundred years.

I repeat that the United States has taken this far-reaching measure not because it fears another war between India and Pakistan; or because it seeks to restrain their arms race; or because it seeks to divert heavy military expenditures for economic development. The official reasons given by the United States Government are meant to clothe the decision with respectability, but the real motives behind this façade of righteousness are as follows:

1. The United States today exercises optimum influence in India and Pakistan and believes that it is in a position to compel both countries simultaneously to an arrangement compatible with its own global interest.

2. The United States wants this arrangement to come into being expeditiously, on account of the growing difficulties it faces in Vietnam, where it thinks that it is engaged in a decisive struggle for its future position in the continent of Asia.

3. It believes the time to be appropriate because of the *détente* between the United States and USSR, which establishes an area of common interest in the sub-continent, and expects that the Soviet Union will desist from exploiting the situation.

4. The United States believes that China is too involved in its internal problems and has received too many setbacks to take any bold counter-initiative.

5. Internal difficulties in India and Pakistan, especially economic and in respect of food supply, are propitious for the application of numerous kinds of pressure on both countries.

6. The United States has tested Indian and Pakistani reactions to pressure and considers it can take a calculated risk in the application of new and severer pressures to accelerate the achievement of its global policies.

It is pertinent to ask why the United States chose to apply coercion in the military field when it has at its disposal numerous economic levers. It cannot be denied that a modicum of pressure from such levers was applied before announcing the decision to terminate military assistance. In fact, many pressures were surreptitiously applied as a prelude to this decision. The United States terminated the agreements under which India and Pakistan receive food on a liberal long-term basis and concluded new agreements with stringent terms which provided food on a month-by-month basis to feed the starving people of India from ship to mouth. The United States also terminated its liberal long-term food deliveries to the sub-continent and, more recently, put both countries virtually on a 'month-by-month' basis. Nor was this the only change. Out of India's total requirement of about 10 million tons of food-grains, she was made to spend only $18 million of foreign exchange on food imports; and out of Pakistan's total requirement of about 2·5 millions, she was made to spend approximately $90 million of her foreign exchange in 1966-7 on food imports. The liberal terms of PL-480 were modified much more adversely for Pakistan at a time when the country faced an acute food shortage. Other pressures were applied in the economic field by the release of economic aid on a piecemeal basis, whereby the strain of uncertainty had an adverse effect on the economic situation generally. However, the enforcement of economic sanctions does not have the same impact as the termination of military assistance, where it threatens a nation's security. Economic difficulties can generally be overcome by internal adjustments. In this instance, the application of sustained economic pressure would have caused greater hardship to India than to Pakistan, on whom the greater pressure has at present to be exerted, as immeasurably more is demanded from Pakistan. Pressure on a nation's food supply can be a powerful lever, but to apply it openly to create famine conditions would have tarnished the image of the United States—a great Christian state, known for its humane traditions. Moreover, if food had been withheld, it would have harmed India much more than Pakistan and, for the reason stated, it was necessary to apply greater pressure on Pakistan.

The stoppage of military assistance has the appearance of a moral gesture and one in accordance with the trend of the times. Ostensibly a decision promoting peace, it suits the spirit of the United Nations with its emphasis on disarmament. In fairness to United States' diplomacy, it must be admitted that less injurious means were attempted before applying this open sanction. It is never a pleasant task to administer obvious pressure and has only now been applied because less blatant attempts failed to register sufficient progress. The decision of 12 April 1967 has been announced in the context of a series of discreet approaches, and there were reports of discussions on joint economic ventures between India and Pakistan under the aegis of the United States. Since 1958, American policy has been directed towards entangling Pakistan with India in a catena of joint ventures, which would subordinate Pakistan. Pursuing this objective, President Johnson, in his message to Congress, waxed eloquent on the virtues of joint regional projects. In New Delhi on 9 May 1967, this theme was elaborated by Mr. George Woods, President of the World Bank, when he stated that numerous advantages would accrue to India and Pakistan if they collaborated in projects that could be financed by the Bank. He went on to say that he had exchanged views with Indian leaders on this matter and, as an example, mentioned the water systems of East Pakistan and West Bengal in India. He showed impatience at the lack of progress on this joint project, observing that preliminary studies on a project for its utilization had been too long delayed. We were also informed of strenuous endeavours made to bring about a bilateral reduction of armed forces. It appears that when the initiatives for joint economic ventures and efforts to bring about reduction of armed forces did not make headway, the United States proceeded to apply pressure where it hurt most.

Joint economic projects between India and Pakistan cannot even be contemplated without the settlement of the Jammu and Kashmir dispute, and without a genuine normalization of relations. Such co-operation can only stem from equality and mutual trust. It cannot be secured at gun-point particularly when one nation has usurped the economic and territorial rights of its neighbour. Under such conditions, it is even less practical to attempt to compel a reduction in the level of their armed forces.

CHAPTER 7

Collaboration with India on American Terms

The reasons adduced for joint economic collaboration between India and Pakistan are precisely those advanced against the Partition of the sub-continent. Arguments, decisively settled by Partition, have been resurrected. The objections of the Indian National Congress to a division of the sub-continent's economy and security forces had been overruled at the creation of Pakistan by the Muslim's decision to be 'separate and equal'. Many years ago, in a conversation between Mr. Jinnah and the British author Beverley Nichols, the economic and defence consequences of Partition were discussed.

SELF [Nichols] The first is economic. Are the Muslims likely to be richer or poorer under Pakistan? And would you set up tariffs against the rest of India?

JINNAH I'll ask you a question for a change. Supposing you were asked which you would prefer . . . a rich England under Germany or a poor England free, what would your answer be?

SELF It's hardly necessary to say.

JINNAH Quite. Well, doesn't that make your question look a little shoddy? This great ideal rises far above mere questions of personal comfort or temporary convenience. The Muslims are a tough people, lean and hardy. If Pakistan means that they will have to be a little tougher, they will not complain. But why *should* it mean that? What conceivable reason is there to suppose that the gift of nationality is going to be an economic liability? A sovereign nation of a hundred million people—even if they are not immediately self-supporting and even if they *are* industrially backward—is hardly likely to be in a worse economic position than if its members are scattered and disorganized, under the dominance of two hundred and fifty million Hindus whose one idea is to exploit them. How any European can get up and say that Pakistan is 'economically impossible' after the Treaty of Versailles is really beyond my comprehension. The great brains who cut Europe into a ridiculous patchwork of conflicting and artificial boundaries are hardly the people to talk economics to us, particularly as our problem happens to be far simpler.

SELF And does that also apply to defence?

JINNAH Of course it applies to defence. Once again I will ask *you* a question. How is Afghanistan defended? Well? The answer is not very complicated. By the Afghans. Just that. We are a brave and united people who are prepared to work and, if necessary, fight. So how does the question of defence present any peculiar difficulties? In what way do we differ from other nations? From Iran, for example? Obviously, there will have to be a transition period. . . .

JINNAH You will remember I said, a moment ago, that the British would have to do a lot of hard thinking. It's a habit they don't find very congenial; they prefer to be comfortable, to wait and see, trusting that everything will come right in the end. However, when they do take the trouble to think, they think as clearly and creatively as any people in the world. And one of their best thinkers—at least on the Indian problem—was old John Bright. Have you ever read any of his speeches?

SELF Not since I left school.

JINNAH Well, take a look at this. I found it by chance the other day.

He handed me the book. It was a faded old volume, *The Speeches of John Bright,* and the date of the page at which it was opened was June 4th, 1858. This is what the greatest orator in the House of Commons said on that occasion:

> '*How long does England propose to govern India? Nobody can answer this question. But be it 50 or 100 or 500 years, does any man with the smallest glimmering of common sense believe that so great a country, with its 20 different nationalities and its 20 different languages, can ever be bounded up and consolidated into one compact and enduring empire confine? I believe such a thing to be utterly impossible.*'

JINNAH What Bright said then is true today . . . In fact, it's far more true—though, of course, the emphasis is not so much on the 20 nationalities as on the 2 . . . the Muslim and the Hindu. And why is it more true? Why hasn't time brought us together? Because the Muslims are *awake* . . . because they've learnt, through bitter experience, the sort of treatment they may expect from the Hindus in a 'United India'. A 'United India' means a Hindu-dominated India. It means that and nothing else. Any other meaning you attempt to impose on it is mythical. 'India' is a British creation . . . it is merely a single administrative unit governed by a bureaucracy under the sanction of the sword. That is all. It is a paper creation, it has no basis in flesh and blood.

SELF The ironical thing is that your critics say that Pakistan itself is a British creation—that it is an example of our genius for applying the principle of 'divide and rule'.

JINNAH (*with some heat*) The man who makes such a suggestion must have a very poor opinion of British intelligence, apart from his opinion of my own integrity. The one thing which *keeps* the British in India is the false idea of a United India, as preached by Gandhi. A United India, I repeat, is a British creation—a myth, and a very dangerous myth, which will cause endless strife. As long as that strife exists, the British have an excuse for remaining. For once in a way, 'divide and rule' does not apply.

SELF What you want is 'divide and quit'?

JINNAH You have put it very neatly.

SELF You realize that all this will come as something of a shock to the British electorate?

JINNAH Truth is often shocking. But why this truth in particular?

SELF Because the average, decent, liberal-minded voter, who wishes Britain to fulfil her pledges, and grant independence to India, has heard nothing but the Congress point of view. The Muslims have hardly a single spokesman in the West.

JINNAH (*bitterly*) I am well aware of that. The Hindus have organized a powerful Press and Congress—Mahasabha are backed up by Hindu capitalists and industrialists with finance which we have not got.

SELF As a result they believe that Congress is 'India', and since Congress never tires of repeating that India is one and indivisible, they imagine that any attempt to divide it is illiberal, reactionary, and generally sinister. They seriously *do* believe this. I know that it is muddle-headed, but then a democracy such as ours, which has to make up its mind on an incredible number of complicated issues, usually is muddle-headed. What they have to learn is that the only liberal course, the only generous course, the only course compatible with a sincere intention to quit India and hand over the reins of government . . .

JINNAH And the only safe course, you might add, is . . .

SELF
JINNAH } Pakistan!

*

The essence of Pakistan—at least of its spirit—is found in the foregoing dialogue. To give a complete exposition of the details of the plan, in a book of this size, would be quite impossible. It would need a sheaf of maps and pages of statistics, and it would carry us far afield, over the borders of India, and involve us in a great deal of unprofitable speculation.

It is fairly certain, however, that the reader who takes the trouble to go really deeply into the matter, with a mind unwarped by prejudice, will come to the conclusion that Pakistan offers no insuperable difficulties, economic, ethnographic, political or strategic, and is likely, indeed, to prove a good deal easier of attainment than a large number of similar problems which the world has successfully resolved in the past fifty years. It is, of course, a major surgical operation, but unfortunately there are occasions in the lives of nations, as of individuals, when major surgical operations are not only desirable but vitally necessary. And this is one of those occasions. The constant friction between the Hindu and Muslim nations has produced something which strongly resembles a cancer in the body politic. There is only one remedy for a cancer, in its advanced stages, and that is the knife. Gandhi's faith cures, British soothing syrup, the ingenious nostrums which are proffered by eager hands throughout the world—all these are useless. They only aggravate the patient's condition and make his ultimate cure more difficult. To the knife it will have to come in the end, and surely one knife, used swiftly and with precision, is better than a million knives, hacking in blind anarchy in the dark?

What is strange, in the whole Pakistan controversy, is not the support which it is slowly gaining among all realistic men but the opposition which it still evokes from sincere well-wishers of India. This is, of course, due to the strength and persistence of Congress propaganda, backed by Hindu big business. The Hindus have almost a monopoly of propaganda. By subtle and persistent suggestion they have managed to persuade the world that they are 'India' and that any attempt to divide 'India' is a wicked 'plot on the part of the British, acting on the well-established principle of divide and rule'.

Most liberals of the West have fallen for this propaganda, hook, line and sinker. Consequently, we have the extraordinary spectacle of 'advanced' British politicians rising to their feet in the House of Commons, and solemnly and sincerely pleading the cause of Indian 'Unity' *in the joint cause of Indian independence*—sublimely ignorant of the fact that their insistence on this so-called 'unity' is the one and only thing that keeps the British in the saddle!

Unite and Rule
Divide and Quit[1]

After two decades of independence, Indo-Pakistan relations have remained static. None of the animosities have been

---

[1] Beverley Nichols, *Verdict on India*, 1944, pp. 190–5.

removed, none of the causes of Partition remedied. In the prevailing conditions, a reduction in the armed forces of India and Pakistan would freeze the disputes for ever and benefit India. It would amount to *de facto* recognition of India's supremacy in the sub-continent and, to all intents and purposes, legalize its usurpation of Pakistan's economic and territorial rights. History holds no example of bilateral disarmament between states with fundamental, unresolved territorial disputes. Disarmament measures have generally been taken under multilateral aegis like the League of Nations or the United Nations. Unilateral disarmament is suicidal. Bilateral disarmament between adversaries is a negation of sovereignty and an admission of defeat by one of them. In the case of India and Pakistan, bilateral disarmament at present is inconceivable. It would be a grave risk to agree to bilateral reduction of forces for all time, when future developments might bring unexpected changes and cause friction over unresolved disputes.

A reduction in armed forces is impracticable for these reasons and for more mundane considerations. It cannot come about by budgetary discipline alone. Nor can it be enforced by Pakistan's having one man in uniform for every three or four Indians in uniform. In a technological age disarmament is no longer as simple as that. It is no more a question of reducing the number of divisions and brigades, but a highly complicated undertaking which has so far not succeeded in producing result in multilateral negotiations. So many factors have to be taken into account that a balance of strength defies arithmetical calculation. In reducing the level of our armed forces, we would have to take into account India's manpower outside her regular forces, her progress in the development of weapons, her advances in nuclear development, her fuel and mineral resources, the number and quality of her factories producing tanks and aircraft and automatic weapons, and the quality of such weapons. These and many other factors have to be calculated in seeking balanced reduction. In addition, there would have to be means of verifying the implementation of such an agreement. India's record in the implementation of past agreements is woefully inadequate. Inspection and control in so vast a country are more difficult than in Pakistan and, even if possible, who is to be the custodian of control? If the custodians are to be the United States and the Soviet Union, it would mean entering into a new phase of the cold war rather than avoiding war; and the whole point of the operation would be lost. China would accuse both countries of submission to United States–Soviet tutelage directed against her.

In spite of the self-evident objections to bilateral disarmament, the Pakistan Government has taken the unusual step of announcing unilateral reduction in the expenditure on armed forces for 1967–8. In presenting his budget, the Finance Minister extolled the virtues of development and expatiated on the burdens of armaments which he considered to be 'non-productive expenditure'. As a 'gesture' to India, the Government reduced the defence expenditure for the current year by Rs. 70 million (from Rs. 2,250 million to Rs. 2,180 million) and imposed a total cut of as much as 24 per cent from the peak defence expenditure of Rs. 2,850 million in 1965–6. Judging from past experience, Pakistan may have to pay very dearly for this gesture. It is a tragic commentary on present official thinking that it has forgotten what price Pakistan had to pay during the September war of 1965 for having virtually frozen its defence expenditure, despite a sharp upward trend in India's defence outlay since 1962. During that war, many Government officials did not conceal their bitter regret at not having increased defence expenditure since 1962 to provide one or two more divisions, which might have made the decisive difference between victory and defeat.

Even the peak expenditure of Rs. 2,850 million in the war year of 1965–6 was barely sufficient to offset the expenditure of over Rs. 10,260 million regularly earmarked by India since 1962. With the termination of military assistance from the United States, it would have been more sensible to maintain, if not increase, the expenditure on defence, which is less than one quarter that of India. In introducing a measure of unilateral disarmament sufficient to have dire consequences on the nation's security, the Government of Pakistan seems to be unaware of the truth of Santayana's observation that 'those who cannot remember the past are condemned to repeat it'.

CHAPTER 8

American Demands and the Choices before Pakistan

The United States' decision to stop military assistance to the sub-continent appears to be directed against both countries in the form of what was called 'even-handed treatment' at the time of the Indo-Pakistan conflict in 1965. Like the earlier treatment, this, in reality, is injurious only to Pakistan, which for over a decade has received military equipment solely from the United States. Her armed forces are accustomed to American weapons and the defence establishment has been orientated according to American thinking. Pakistan does not possess sufficient indigenous ordnance factories for its ammunition requirements, nor does it have a steel mill or factories producing armaments. Although, all of a sudden, Pakistan's one source of military supplies has dried up, the United States' decision provoked an uproar in India. Under certain stringent conditions, the United States has agreed to permit the sale of spare parts on a cash basis to both countries. This concession, admittedly, will cushion Pakistan's defence requirements for a brief period. It has been made, however, not to give Pakistan any passing advantage over India, but to continue to maintain the American hold on Pakistan's defence machinery. It is in the United States' interest to keep a finger on the trigger even after the termination of its military assistance. Not only does it thereby retain its influence in this most vital field, but it can also extract valuable information concerning the military equipment Pakistan has recently received from other sources.

If Pakistan does not now hasten to take positive counter-measures to safeguard her security, India is likely to evict more Muslims on the Assam borders, take over East Pakistan's water resources, strangle its economy, and prepare to launch an attack on Azad Kashmir and, if necessary, on the rest of Pakistan.

Internal disorders and external difficulties might well tempt India to make such an attack. Aggression has now become an established instrument of India's foreign policy, an instrument employed on no less than six occasions since her Independence twenty years ago. If the military balance is to swing in India's favour, there is no reason to suppose that she would hesitate to commit aggression for the seventh time and strike at Pakistan, her 'enemy number one'.

To turn now to the United States' other sub-continental objectives, there is sufficient evidence on record to establish that the Anglo-American Powers wanted a united India to face the 'historical threat' of Russia to the sub-continent and their control of the Indian Ocean. They accepted Partition reluctantly and, at that time, did much to strengthen India in the hope and expectation that, when the passions of the moment had died down, the two peoples would come together again. After Independence the United States made many overtures to India and, only when it became clear that Prime Minister Nehru was not prepared to involve India in Great Power politics and become a pawn in the global struggle, was Pakistan inveigled into the pacts in 1954 and military assistance extended. After 1962 the whole situation changed. The United States saw a great opportunity to step into India and win it over to its sphere of influence. In the expectation that it would ultimately be able to lever Pakistan into a position of co-operation with India the United States warmly applauded the proposal of joint defence and subsequently made many strenuous efforts to promote collaboration between India and Pakistan.

As a result of these changed conditions, the United States sees the Jammu and Kashmir dispute in a different light. It is for this reason that United Nations resolutions calling for the exercise of the right of self-determination by the people of Jammu and Kashmir have faded into the background. There can be no fairer way to resolve such a dispute than to ascertain the wishes of the people, but the United States now regards this problem as an embarrassing obstruction in the realization of its plan to encircle China. It has to consider India's need to hold the Kashmir valley with its lines of communication to the sensitive region of Ladakh. If this dispute were to be resolved on an equitable basis, it would, in all probability, lead to a peaceful boundary settlement between Pakistan and China. The United States, however, requires not peace on the frontiers with China, but tension to pin down China's military forces from the borders of Manchuria to Ladakh. It would suit American interests for the dispute to be absorbed in a larger overall settlement between India and Pakistan. This would permit the tension on the frontiers to continue with greater intensity and with a united military presence. If the dispute has to be frozen, the termination of military assistance to Pakistan and the resultant military imbalance between India and Pakistan can only help to perpetuate the unjust *status quo*.

It may be asked why India should be reluctant to come to so advantageous a settlement. If Indo-Pakistani co-operation were the exclusive aim of the United States, there would be no reason at all for India to object. If that aim was only to bring about maximum co-operation between India and Pakistan for its own sake, India would experience a sense of triumph; but the attempt to bring about this co-operation is not for its own sake but to encircle China. Having had experience of a minor conflict with China, India is fearful of provoking a hostile confrontation and in normal circumstances would want to maintain a position of non-alignment. She has to contend, however, with the legacy of the Sino-Indian dispute and take into account her present economic and military dependence on the United States and her food-grain requirements, which the United States alone can supply and without which millions of Indians would starve to death. But for these conditions, in all probability India would have sought an adjustment with China. Whether she now wants or does not want such a settlement is irrelevant. What is relevant is that India certainly does not want to aggravate her differences with China and become a pawn in the global conflict. It is one thing to live with the legacy of a border conflict and extract substantial concessions out of the United States by exploiting and exaggerating the border tension. It is quite another to become party to an arrangement which might spell total disaster for the sub-continent. The Vietnam war might well extend beyond its present frontiers. Were that to happen, the attitude of India and Pakistan would be of very great importance and, naturally, India does not want to be involved in such an entanglement. She has followed a policy of non-alignment, but circumstances have put her in a posture of double-alignment. Her resistance to co-operation with Pakistan arises not out of the co-operation *per se*, which is her historical mission, but because this kind of co-operation can only lead to entanglement in global politics. For this reason, India would hesitate and pressure must therefore be exerted on her, but to a lesser degree than on Pakistan. If India succumbs, she is still a doubtful beneficiary. To succeed, where Gandhi and Nehru failed, in securing Pakistan's subservience would be a stimulant to the demoralized people of India and would, perhaps, temporarily arrest internal fissiparous tendencies; but, in return, to be called upon to face China as a belligerent in the global struggle would be a poor exchange. Despite the advantages of such an arrangement, India is likely to consider her consequent entanglement in the United States' global strategy is too high a price to pay for these benefits; in which case she would be subjected to further pressure.

For Pakistan, however, the sacrifice would be twofold. The idea of becoming subservient to India is abhorrent and that of co-operation with India, with the object of provoking tension with China, equally repugnant. Such an arrangement as the United States Government has in mind has both advantages and disadvantages for India; but for Pakistan only disadvantages. If India, notwithstanding her differences with China, is reluctant to become a party in a major conflict with China, it is all the more necessary for Pakistan to avoid a fatal conflict with a country that gave proof of its friendship by coming to our assistance when we faced aggression from India. It would be catastrophic for Pakistan to be dragged into such an alignment.

America's reason for terminating military aid is to force both countries into confrontation with China. Indo-Pakistani co-operation is a necessary step towards a fixed objective, which is the encirclement of China. The United States, being badly bogged down in Vietnam, would like to give military assistance only to countries willing to use that assistance in the Vietnam war and prepared to use it against China. It does not want to waste its weapons and munitions on countries which might use them in conflicts in which the United States is not engaged. Mr. McNamara announced in the spring of 1967 that the Asian

3 The author with President Soekarno in Djakarta, June 1966

countries which will receive the bulk of United States' military assistance—apart from South Vietnam—will be South Korea, Thailand, Philippines, and Taiwan. All are involved in the Vietnam conflict and are co-operating with the United States' armed forces in one form or another.

Apart from the message the decision is intended to convey to India and Pakistan, it seems a sensible policy to supply armaments only to those countries engaged in the Vietnam war and not to countries which are not prepared to use them in this common struggle. Whatever the known prejudice against partition and however unrelaxing the effort in pursuit of a subcontinent united against Communist China, and whatever the changes brought about during the Kennedy administration by the placing of greater emphasis on economic assistance in contradistinction to military alliances, the pragmatic and compelling reason for the suspension of military assistance is to be found in the vicissitudes of Vietnam. With the understandable exception of Israel, which is, in a fundamental sense, both a domestic and an international responsibility of the United States, military equipment is supplied to be used against Communism and not in non-Communist conflicts. This is the crux of the matter. Since the end of the Second World War, the United States has only given military assistance to those countries which are prepared to join in alliance against Communist states. Western Europe was given massive economic and military assistance to become a powerful bastion against the Soviet Union. Military alliances were forged in Asia for the same purpose. Japan, Philippines, Taiwan, South Korea, Thailand, and South Vietnam were given military assistance to confront the People's Republic of China. Iran, Turkey, and Greece were given military assistance to become powerful fortresses against the Soviet Union. Pakistan was armed on condition that she, like other countries in Asia, Europe, and Latin America, entered into alliance in recognition of the Communist danger and would be prepared to be a part of the world-wide encirclement of the Soviet Union and China with the common and collective purpose of containing Communism, if necessary, with the use of force.

The assumption was that Pakistan, being an ideological state, was a natural opponent of godless Communism and, as

H

such, a natural friend of the United States. It was well known that Pakistan had fundamental disputes with India and there was the fear that Pakistan was seeking military assistance only in order to buttress her defences against India. This doubt was always present in the thinking of the United States, but there was the contrary hope that, with the passage of time, Indo-Pakistani differences would resolve themselves and Pakistan would give undivided attention to the Communist threat. This hope seemed to be justified in view of Pakistan's many acts in support of the United States; and in view of Prime Minister Nehru's attitude and declarations, which appeared to the United States to further Communist interests. To demonstrate Pakistan's sincerity and our attachment to the common interest, we deliberately pursued a policy of aloofness towards the Soviet Union and the People's Republic of China. Our relations with the Soviet Union were virtually non-existent. Prime Minister Liaquat Ali Khan abruptly cancelled his visit to the Soviet Union after having sought and received an invitation. This unwarranted step could hardly have contributed to good relations. Many strains developed in our relations with that Great Power until a climax was reached with the U-2 episode.

Pakistan had recognized China after the revolution, but our relations with that country were far from normal. Admittedly, there was an exchange of visits between Prime Ministers on one occasion and some trade contacts, but relations were not satisfactory. Having initially supported China's admission to the United Nations, we later reversed our attitude under pressure from the United States. We were also responsible for some unwarranted provocations during the Korean conflict, so that before 1962 relations between the two countries could not be described as cordial. In the United Nations and other international forums, Pakistan was generally prominent in support of United States' policies, at times with embarrassing fidelity. It was therefore believed that, although India was Pakistan's traditional antagonist, Pakistan nevertheless remained faithful to the United States as its natural friend in the fulfilment of its global policies directed against Communism. To this extent, there was no contradiction in Pakistan's relations with the United States, and we continued to receive military assistance as an ally in a common cause against a common enemy. In reality, however, there was a fundamental contradiction between the assumption under which the United States entered into special relations with Pakistan and Pakistan's own aims. The United States recognized the risks involved in arming Pakistan, but it nevertheless rendered military assistance for the following reasons:

1. It believed that Indo-Pakistani disputes would sooner or later be resolved under the compulsion of geography and of economic and other factors.
2. It believed that, with the increase of its influence in the sub-continent, it would assist the two countries to come to terms.
3. It believed that, if India and Pakistan resolved their differences, Pakistan at least would play its part in the struggle against Communism.
4. Pakistan had an ideology different from Communism, and a conservative leadership was in firm control of the country.
5. Pakistan had sufficiently demonstrated its antipathy to Communism internally and externally.
6. It planned to give military assistance in such a way as to retain effective control over its weapons so that, if Pakistan 'misused' the equipment, the United States could quickly frustrate the venture.

Assistance was provided to Pakistan for one set of reasons and received for another. To this contradiction the Sino-Indian conflict of 1962 added an entirely new element. Nehru ceased to be an antagonist of the United States. In despair and disillusion, he pleaded for American military assistance to rescue himself from the talons of Communist China. It was non-aligned India, and not aligned Pakistan, that had joined battle with America's chief adversary. This new development offered limitless opportunities to the United States for penetrating India in order to bring that country gradually into an arrangement directed against China, which, by this time, had become the United States' principal adversary. This altered situation revealed the irreconcilable contradictions between the different assumptions on which Pakistan and the United States had built their special relations.

For the first time during this period, genuine measures were taken by Pakistan to improve relations with China and, to a lesser extent, with the Soviet Union. With these new developments taking shape, it would have been both naive and unrealistic to expect the United States to continue rendering military assistance to Pakistan for an indefinite period of time. Imperceptibly, events were moving Pakistan towards a final choice. We had either to forsake our fundamental national interests and become hostile to China and continue to qualify for military assistance; or improve relations with China and maintain the struggle for the attainment of our vital national interests at the risk of the suspension of American military assistance. Let us for the moment consider the consequences of acquiescing to the United States' global interest.

In exploring the possibilities available in capitulation by instalment, it must be remembered that it is a function of diplomacy to look for various approaches and to avoid abrupt decisions which sound like ultimatums. What is important is the implementation of policy and the direction it takes. Change comes about gradually and imperceptibly; often, under the cover of emphatic denials. It is like sowing seed for a harvest which will mature only in its natural period. In the present instance, acquiescence could be given over a period of time to any of the following alternatives:

1. Agreement to co-operate with India in an overall settlement, with the disputes absorbed in the larger settlement and jointly to confront China.
2. A secret compromise with the United States and with India on terms of co-operation in the larger context, gaining time to prepare the people of Pakistan for its acceptance.
3. Agreement to co-operate with India against China, provided the United States were to use its influence to bring about an honourable and just settlement of disputes between India and Pakistan.
4. An inequitable settlement with India, not involving Pakistan in confrontation with China.
5. No overall and inequitable settlement with India, but agreement to treat China as an antagonist, independently, as was the position before 1962.

Within the framework of the United States' global objectives, there is little to choose between any of these alternatives. Only outside the sphere of Global Power politics can Pakistan find freedom of action leading to other, and more beneficial, conclusions.

Let us consider the implications of each available choice:

1. From the United States' point of view, the ideal solution would be for Pakistan to co-operate with India in an overall settlement with the disputes absorbed in the larger settlement and collectively to face China. Conversely, this arrangement would be the most damaging to Pakistan, involving an abject surrender to India, a betrayal of values which have been sacrosanct for centuries. It would, moreover, result in enmity with a powerful and friendly neighbour which came to Pakistan's assistance in her hour of greatest peril. Instead of reducing tension, this solution would multiply tensions and create a host of internal problems. It could bring the flames of war into our homes and, were the Vietnam war to spread, it might involve our country in a war of total destruction. An agreement on such terms would not only be humiliating and dangerous, but would provide no material compensations.

2. It would not be possible to keep such a deplorable compromise secret, nor would it serve the United States' interest to maintain the secrecy for long. Moreover, the revelation of such a compromise would cause consternation and be violently opposed by the people of Pakistan.

3. The United States could be told that, as a *quid pro quo* for the resumption of military assistance, Pakistan would co-operate with India against China provided the United States exerted its influence on India to agree to an honourable settlement of all disputes. In such an event, the United States is likely to assure Pakistan that it would make renewed efforts for a fair settlement but, at the same time, caution Pakistan that it is not in a position to force India to relinquish Jammu and Kashmir. Were such vague and ambivalent assurances to be offered, Pakistan should remember the bitter experience of the past; and remember, too, that it might not be in the United States' interest to disturb the *status quo* in Jammu and Kashmir, in view of the Sino-Indian dispute over Ladakh. Pakistan would be entrapped by such a commitment and the disputes would

remain unsettled on a satisfactory basis. If, in such conditions, military assistance is resumed to Pakistan, India would also become eligible. That country's own internal resources and capacity for the production of armaments, coupled with the ever-flowing military supplies from the Soviet Union and Eastern Europe together with the restored assistance from the United States, would soon tilt the military balance between India and Pakistan steeply in India's favour. This would end all chance of an honourable settlement of disputes with India, and, in a few years, India would be in a commanding position to attack Pakistan. In such a situation China, not unaware of Pakistan's changed posture, would be unlikely to respond sympathetically to Pakistan's difficulties.

The restoration of military assistance in such circumstances would be of no avail. It would be brought to a grinding halt—as in the last conflict—if it were used in defence against India, but with the difference that, on this occasion, China would also be hostile. Such an undertaking would achieve not the encirclement of China, but of Pakistan. It would maintain the enmity of India from the south and of China from the north and the east; and, from what may be gathered from recent newspaper reports, it would influence the attitude of Afghanistan as well. Such would be the position in the event of renewed hostilities between India and Pakistan.

The influx of military equipment at the present, or any foreseeable, level would be insufficient to defend Pakistan against China or the Soviet Union. To the objections regarding the inadequate quantum of military equipment for defence against these Powers, the United States has always maintained that, in the event of a full-scale armed conflict, it would itself step in with its military might and consider the use of ultimate weapons. After Vietnam, however, there can be no certainty that the United States will ever again commit its ground forces in vast numbers on the land-mass of Asia. If, moreover, there were any certainty in the use of ultimate weapons, President de Gaulle would not have made his bold departure from the integrated defence system of Western Europe and the Atlantic alliance to give France an independent nuclear deterrent. If Europe, the mother of the United States, is uncertain about the use of nuclear weapons by the United States for the defence of Europe, it is all the more necessary for Asia to be sceptical. In any event, to contribute to a situation that would invite nuclear weapons to our territory, would make us the planners of our own destruction. In the one contingency, we would not be in a position to use effectively the military assistance against India, which is our adversary, and from whom we fear attack; and in the other, that is in the event of its use against China or the Soviet Union, it might lead to the annihilation of our country. So, in either case, the restoration of the *status quo* as it existed before 1962 would have disastrous consquences. Submission to such terms would mean a spiral of tension in times of peace and destruction in times of war. We would surround ourselves with powerful adversaries were we to rely on the nebulous assurance that, if we went to war with the nuclear giants, our friend across the seven seas would be at our bidding. The United States might offer such an assurance, because it is a step in the attainment of its objective, but if it restored military assistance on such terms there would be still more strings attached to it. The United States believes that Pakistan's recent actions have worked against the interest of its global policies. Seeking to bring it back to heel, it would like to ensure that Pakistan does not again get out of hand. So any assurances that Pakistan gets, and any assurances that Pakistan gives, will not automatically restore confidence. Our country will be made to demonstrate its *bona fides* time in and time out, till it leads to our isolation and total dependence.

4. If Pakistan agrees to a settlement with India without agreeing to face China, this would be acceptable to the United States, whom it would give an opportunity to move step by step from one favourable position to another. In these circumstances also, the United States might restore military assistance to both countries, ensuring, however, that co-operation between them will, in due course, become total and that its own increasing influence in the sub-continent will eventually enable it to attain its principal objective. This arrangement would be acceptable to India if the understanding goes no further, but agreeable to the United States only as an interim position. Even if Pakistan unequivocally made it clear that such co-operation would not be employed against China, it would not enjoy any credence in that country. The confidence gained so assiduously

would be lost and China would assume that the change of policy has been made with the eventual object of encircling it. Thus, even in such a situation, Pakistan would arouse the suspicions of China and find herself in compromising situation after situation.

Pakistan's diplomacy will meet its severest test in resisting this arrangement. The terms of the alternatives have the approval of both India and the United States. It is here that the parallel interests of the United States and India converge and, therefore, Pakistan must exercise the utmost vigilance to frustrate the manœuvres, as, in the ultimate analysis, they lead to the same results.

5. Pakistan can agree to continue to treat China as an antagonist as was the position up to 1962, but not co-operate with India in the absence of an honourable settlement of disputes. In the course of time, the United States has found this situation to be unsatisfactory. So long as Indo-Pakistani differences exist it is difficult for the United States to work with any degree of certainty in this region. There are too many imponderables in the situation. Such an agreement would harm it and is one which has already failed. What the United States wants is the maximum effective encirclement of China, for which neither Pakistan nor India is alone sufficient; their collaboration is essential. But even if the United States agrees to such an accommodation, it will continue to make efforts to bring about the co-operation between India and Pakistan for its global interest, especially in view of the strategic difficulties in the eastern wing of the sub-continent, where only a narrow strip of a few miles separates Pakistan from Assam and the Himalayan states. Without the co-operation of Pakistan this whole region is extremely vulnerable to armed penetration. Such an agreement would result in renewed antagonism between China and Pakistan and the continuance of existing tensions between India and Pakistan, a situation which Afghanistan is not likely to ignore. It would again bring about the encirclement of Pakistan and increase the number of its adversaries from one to three. Nor would that be the end of the story. If we agree to such terms, Pakistan would be called upon to make a token contribution in the Vietnam war. The moment Pakistan agrees to make any contribution to the United States'

military effort in Vietnam, it will make itself eligible for military assistance, but this would mean an irreconcilable conflict with China. It would not only be an action against the current of history, alien to the movement of our times, but it might also encourage India to become more hostile in the hope of provoking an open quarrel between China and Pakistan. The Soviet Union and China and, indeed, all Socialist and non-aligned States would regard us as mercenaries engaged against fellow Asians in a barbaric and unjust war.

All five choices are unacceptable to Pakistan. In one way or another, all lead to the same fatal consequences. This does not mean that Pakistan does not want a settlement with India; indeed, Pakistan fervently seeks peace with India, but the settlement must be honourable and on the basis of equality. Once the disputes are resolved in a spirit of understanding and according to norms of justice, Pakistan would be prepared to co-operate with India on terms of mutual benefit. However, this co-operation must be between two sovereign independent nations and not dictated by Global Powers for their own ends. India and Pakistan must be left free to shape their own futures in peace. If their disputes are resolved honourably, outside the interplay of global politics, no one in Pakistan will object to co-operation between the two nations.

In analysing the implications of military assistance, a balance sheet has to be drawn up of gains and losses. The cessation of aid has both advantages and drawbacks. It can be interpreted as a development which has saved Pakistan from being engulfed in a deplorable Asian or global war. If we refuse to use arms against the Soviet Union and China, those Global Powers have a corresponding obligation not to use their arms against us. It would remove sources of suspicion and conflict between Pakistan and its two powerful northern neighbours. It would permit Pakistan to give its undivided attention and resources to meet the one and only genuine threat to its security and territorial integrity. The question is how Pakistan can adequately meet this threat to its security in the absence of renewed military assistance from the United States. While it is true that military assistance was not made available for use against India, nevertheless its possession did act as a deterrent against India. In the last war, Pakistan was able to use the United States' military assistance until the United States imposed an embargo and other restrictions.

The question now to be answered is how is this deterrent to be maintained?

CHAPTER 9

The Indo-Pakistan War and its Analogies

The ways in which Pakistan can meet the challenge to her vital interests can best be considered by seeing how she stands in the world. Indeed, an assessment of Pakistan's international position and her attitude to world issues is of paramount importance in evaluating how she will be able to resist foreign intervention in her internal affairs.

To some extent the policies of the United States and India run parallel, but fortunately for Pakistan their ultimate objectives differ. In the interest of its sovereignty, it is essential for Pakistan to conduct its diplomacy in such a way as to divide the parallel lines and enlarge the contradictions. India seeks to bring Pakistan back to Mother India, but is not anxious to become entangled in a global conflict against China. The United States wants to see meaningful co-operation between India and Pakistan with the purpose of encircling China and, if this is to be the purpose, India would hesitate to have that kind of co-operation with Pakistan. India would equally resent the growing interference in her internal affairs aimed at making her an active instrument in the cold war.

Pakistan has no alternative but to resist foreign interference inimical to her national interest and to carry on the struggle for the vindication of its legitimate rights in the sub-continent. The success or failure of her diplomacy will depend not only on her bilateral and direct relations with India, on the one hand, and with the United States on the other, and with them jointly, but on the manner in which she discharges her international obligations and conducts her general foreign policy.

Although the principal challenge to Pakistan comes from India and the brunt of the international pressure from the United States, it would be wrong to lose sight of the rest of the world in this context. Just as it was necessary to trace the evolution of United States' relations with Pakistan in order to interpret properly that country's recent actions affecting Pakistan, it is equally necessary for Pakistan to define and determine her place in the world, in Asia, and in the sub-continent, for meeting the challenge of the times.

Pakistan has a moral obligation to support de-colonization and to strive for a more equitable economic and social international order. Afro-Asian unity is a powerful force for emancipation and Pakistan, as a member of the Afro-Asian community, has to be in the vanguard of the Afro-Asian movement. It can be justly demanded from Pakistan that she should continue to identify herself with the aspirations of the peoples of these continents. Like us, most of Asia and Africa was in bondage for centuries. As a newly independent country, it is our bounden duty to accelerate the progress of freedom and economic emancipation. We cannot expect other states to support us in our righteous cause if we are reluctant to put our weight behind the just causes of others. It is only when we are prepared to share in the common struggle and exercise our influence in a spirit of comradeship and equality that we can expect to enhance our prestige and find increased support for ourselves. Afro-Asian solidarity is neither a myth nor an abstract philosophy, but a condition necessary both for our individual advancement as well as our collective protection. The underdeveloped nations, the bulk of which are in Asia and Africa, are the proletarian nations of the world. Though individually they may be as weak and impoverished as is a single workman or peasant, together they are as formidable as a collective movement of the labouring masses.

So far, Pakistan has been able to identify herself with the aspirations of Asia and Africa and our support for these countries has been of significant advantage to us. In Asia and Africa, as in Europe, there are certain key states which require Pakistan's particular attention. In Africa she must cultivate better relations with the French-speaking countries, as well as with Muslim states and Commonwealth nations; and in Asia, we must concentrate our attention on our neighbours and such countries as Japan, Cambodia, and the heroic nation of Vietnam, which deserves our special sympathy.

Japan is the most prosperous country in Asia on account of its highly developed economy. Like the Federal Republic of

Germany, it is at present under heavy American influence. In many ways it is the most important country in Asia as regards the United States' grand strategy against China. For years after the Second World War the Japanese took little part in international affairs, but are now increasingly exerting their influence in Asian and world affairs. However, Japanese interests are not likely to deviate from those of the United States for a long time. To give one example, Japan refused to allow Pakistan International Airlines to touch Tokyo in continuation of its flights to Canton and Shanghai. We must learn to live with such problems and be patient, for it is essential that we improve our economic and cultural co-operation with Japan; and if, in the meantime, we cannot get Japanese support, we should try to assure their neutrality in questions important to us.

Pakistan has a primary responsibility to foster comrade-ship among Muslim nations in accordance with its traditional foreign policy, which derives from the obligations imposed by the country's Constitution and ideology. We share with the Muslim states stretching from Morocco to Indonesia a number of affinities, and even before Independence, Muslims of the sub-continent gave what support they could to Islamic causes. This movement of solidarity is a factor which cannot be ignored by the Great and Global Powers in the formulation of their policies. Although Pakistan's policy has always been to develop the friendliest possible relations with Muslim countries, she has on occasions encountered difficulties. There have been failures, which can be ascribed partly to our lack of experience in international affairs and partly to the internecine conflicts of the Middle East.

The traditional problems of the Middle East always appear to be colossal, but they have been surpassed by those introduced with the Arab–Israel war of June 1967. This brief conflict has, temporarily at least, changed the map of the region and radically altered the balance of power. It has done incalculable harm to the Arab peoples, but the sting of defeat may provide their leaders with a final opportunity to rally and remedy the wrongs they have suffered. Internal Arab disputes, which were getting more and more complicated, can perhaps now be smoothed out. One of the main causes of antagonism between the Arab states lies in their conflicting social systems, but, if Capitalism and Communism can co-exist, it should not be beyond the reach of human endeavour to establish a working accommodation between Arab socialism and Arab conservatism; especially as Islam, language, and geography form permanent links of cohesion. The scars of war and the need to redress the consequences of defeat should furnish the incentive for an urgently needed *modus vivendi* between the Arab socialist and conservative regimes. Since the United Arab Republic occupies a special place in the Arab World and in Africa, and for other obvious reasons too, Pakistan should cultivate its relations with that country. This need not be inconsistent with her cordial relations with Saudi Arabia and other Arab states. The war in the Yemen has bedevilled inter-Arab relations and must be brought to an early end to permit Arab unity to counter the threat of Israel. Had Arab forces not been engaged in such large numbers in the Yemen, they could have been deployed to better use against Israel in the last war.

The tragedy of this futile war in the Yemen is that a treaty to terminate hostilities, called the Jeddah Agreement, already exists between the United Arab Republic and Saudi Arabia; but although it has been in existence for over a year, there has been not the slightest movement towards its implementation. It could in no way be construed as an act of interference if friendly states were to urge the implementation of an agreement which has already been voluntarily arrived at by the two states. If the war in the Yemen does not come to an end and if the disorders in Aden and its surrounding territories become more serious, this sensitive region could become the cockpit of a bitter conflict involving not only an enlarged quarrel between Muslim states, but also attracting Great Power intervention. The Arabs do not need to be told what it means to invite Great Power intervention. Even before the Arab–Israel war, the interference of Great Powers in their region had caused them innumerable difficulties. There are many ways of resisting the interference of Great and Global Powers: one is to remove the conditions which attract their intervention. The problems of the Gulf region will have to be looked at anew by the Arab states in order to eliminate intervention by the Great Powers and to prevent regional tensions. What is needed is to prevent the plunder of the fabulous wealth of the poverty-stricken people of the region. Federations of the sheikhs are being considered to facilitate collective exploitation. The blessing of freedom does not create a void. On the contrary, a free people are the best guardians of their rights. The theory of 'political vacuum' is a product of neo-colonialism, and the departure of the British will create no such vacuum. The people of the Persian Gulf region will have to resolve their differences like a truly independent people unwarped by the prejudices left behind by colonialism. Pakistan must keep a vigilant eye on such potential trouble spots; for circumstances could place her on the horns of a dilemma. She must work for the reduction of tensions and make what contributions she can towards shaping peaceful co-existence among fraternal Islamic states.

The internal Arab quarrels, the conflict in the Yemen, and the rivalries between progressive and conservative regimes in the Arab world, have all been overtaken by the Middle East war of June 1967. No event since the end of the Second World War has caused greater territorial changes. It has called in question the *raison d'être* of the balance of terror between the Global Powers and given substance to China's criticism of the doctrine of co-existence.

In considering these events, it is important to make comparisons and learn their lessons. Before unleashing its aggression on Pakistan, India conducted some probing military operations in the Rann of Kutch to test Pakistan's resolve in resisting encroachments on her territory. Similarly, Israel conducted probing operations against Jordan in November 1966 and against Syria before embarking on aggression. Prime Minister Shastri and the Israeli Prime Minister Levi Eshkol chose exactly the same words with which to threaten the victims of aggression, saying that they would attack at a time and place of their choosing. In both the Indo-Pakistan war and the conflict between Israel and the Arab states, aggression was committed by the usurpers of territory. Even so, some Western Powers were critical of the victims of aggression for acts of war, forgetting that the United Nations Charter provides for self-defence and general international law permits wars of liberation under the well-established doctrine of *Bellum Justum*. Just as Pakistan did not immediately come to the aid of the freedom fighters in Jammu and Kashmir, the Arab states also did not carry their action to a logical conclusion after closing the Gulf of Aqaba, as they had a right to do under international law. Neither Pakistan nor the Arab states completed the plain exercise of their rights, and all suffered as a result. In both cases the initiative was left to the aggressors, who took the fullest advantage by striking first with all their might. In the Indo-Pakistan war, the Air Force of Pakistan gained mastery of the skies and this supremacy had its effect on the fortunes of the war. In the Middle Eastern conflict, Israel with its surprise attack gained the decisive air superiority. In both wars the aggressors violated cease-fire agreements and occupied strategic territories after the cease-fire; in both, sanctions were threatened by the Global Powers. After the Indo-Pakistan war, the Indians committed genocide in Kashmir, driving Muslims from their homes and replacing them by Hindu Dogra populations. Similarly, Israel has now begun to evict Arabs from the territories they occupied and is calling for fresh Jewish immigration from other countries in order to replace the indigenous population and to reduce the Arab majority into a minority.

The Great Powers' attitudes displayed even more striking similarities. The United States proclaimed its neutrality in the Indo-Pakistan war, but in the event its attitude caused difficulty to Pakistan. Similarly, in the Arab–Israel war it proclaimed its neutrality, but was sympathetic to Israel. After the ultimatum given to India by the People's Republic of China, the Anglo-American Powers threatened Pakistan with dire consequences; and a few days before the Irsaeli attack the American Ambassador to Cairo made a *démarche* to President Nasser. In both conflicts, the United States and the Soviet Union co-operated in the United Nations and demanded cease-fires. Under cover of the Security Council the United States and the Soviet Union got together to hammer out a resolution to put an end to hostilities without settling the merits of the disputes. Commenting on the effect this co-operation had, Senator Fulbright says:

Soviet-American co-operation in bringing about the cease-fire in the India-Pakistan war in September 1965 is one example of the kind of beneficial collaboration that the Vietnamese war makes increasingly difficult. That co-operation—or 'parallelism', as it was called—was possible because the Kashmir war was one of the very

4 The author with President Podgorny in Moscow, June 1965

few international conflicts of the postwar era, and perhaps the most important, in relation to which Russia and America had similar interests. As a result of their shared interest in a cease-fire that would humiliate neither India nor Pakistan while also having the effect of restraining China, the Soviet Union and the United States brought decisive influence to bear for the acceptance by both sides of the United Nations Security Council cease-fire resolution.

The interplay of Global Powers working in unison behind the screen of the United Nations to produce resolutions on the Middle East was strikingly reminiscent of the treatment given to Kashmir from the time of the first conflict twenty years ago to the day when the Security Council again demanded another cease-fire in September 1965. The same story is being written again with unimaginative repetition. The same man, Gunnar Jaring, carrying the same brief-case, has been dispatched to the capitals of the Middle East in the same way in which he travelled between India and Pakistan little less than a decade ago. The Secretary-General of the United Nations was deputed in both instances to plead for a cease-fire and the United Nations was used as a cover by the Super-Powers to co-ordinate their policies. In both the wars, once agreement was reached between the Super-Powers, the Security Council demanded a cease-fire and threatened sanctions. In both the wars, the Soviet Union did not want the hostilities to be enlarged into a conflict of the Great Powers and for this reason was anxious to terminate them at all costs. In the Arab–Israel war, the Soviet Union took a wavering position as it did in the Indo-Pakistan war and, in the final analysis, in both cases, it collaborated with the United States to enforce their common will. In the search for peace, France played a commendable role in both conflicts by looking beyond mere cease-fires, while Britain in both stood behind the United States. As in the case of the Indo-Pakistan war, it is being suggested that the United Nations' resolution for the withdrawal of Israeli forces can only be effective with Anglo-American and Soviet collaboration; and, again, that if the United Nations are unable to effect a settlement, the four Great Powers, excluding China, should make an attempt to secure peace in the Middle East. China came out with unqualified support for the victims of aggression in both wars, as did the bulk of the Third World. Soon after the Indo-Pakistan war

came to an end, the United States became active in pressing
Pakistan and India to collaborate on joint economic ventures.
Hardly has the smell of cordite disappeared from the Middle
Eastern battlefield, when obtuse suggestions of joint economic
collaboration between Israel and the Arab states are emanating
from the United States. As in the case of India and Pakistan,
the benefits of sharing the river waters are being extolled in the
Middle East. After a reappraisal of policy, in April 1967, the
United States terminated its military aid to Pakistan and India.
Now the House of Representatives Foreign Affairs Committee
is reported to be considering the establishment of sub-com-
mittees to study American Aid to the Middle East, and it has
been suggested that the Great Powers should collaborate to
limit armaments to the Middle East. In both cases, the United
States is insisting on 'an overall settlement' between the belli-
gerents. Perhaps the most important similarity between the two
situations was the dark shadow of the Vietnam war, which para-
doxically provided both the opportunity for starting the wars
and the compulsion for bringing them to a rapid end.

The points of difference are of equal interest, in so far as
they illustrate even more fully the complex realities of the international situation. The most significant difference between
Pakistan's situation and that of the Arab states appears in the
fact that, while China supported us unequivocally and without
reservations and, as an immediate neighbour, was in a position
effectively to implement its ultimatum, the Soviet support to
the Arab World turned out to be disappointing at the height
of the war. On the military side, shortly before the cease-fire
Pakistan was better placed; whereas in the Arab–Israel war,
Israel had attained its military objectives and was still advancing when the cease-fire was agreed upon.

Events, if they are properly controlled, and opportunities, if
they are properly grasped, will put an end to Britain's 'East of
Suez' role. The United States, in spite of its successes, has
damaged its long-term position in the Middle East. The prestige of the Soviet Union has suffered and, unless it stages a
spectacular come-back with massive military assistance and
other measures of tangible support, its position in the Arab
World is unlikely to recover quickly. It is reported that Cuba
charged the Soviet Union with 'scandalous capitulation'. In an

attempt to repair the damage to Soviet prestige, diplomatic relations with Israel were severed, the Russian Prime Minister went to the General Assembly, and the President to Cairo, Damascus, and Baghdad; but unless the Soviet Union succeeds in making Israel relinquish captured territory, and takes other concomitant steps to reassert its claim to world leadership, its prestige will not easily be restored. There was disillusionment in Arab countries over the attitude of the Soviet Union to their war with Israel. The explanation given for the Russian compromise was that its intervention would have led to a Third World War. Had another world war taken place, it would not have been confined to the destruction of the Soviet Union. If the Anglo-American Powers were prepared to face these consequences, or at least give the impression that they would face them in the fulfilment of their commitments to Israel, the change in the Soviet Union's attitude cannot be explained away on the ground that its intervention on behalf of the Arab states would have led to a major war. The truth of the matter is that the Soviet Union cannot continue to make one compromise after another without relinquishing its claims to the leadership of revolutionary causes. There is little room left for any further accommodation. Russia must either re-establish her authority as the protector of oppressed peoples' just causes, even if the fulfilment of this responsibility carries the risk of war, or forsake her commanding position in international affairs.

It has been a long road from the militant and uncompromising attitude of Stalin to Khrushchev's spirit of Camp David and now to Prime Minister Kosygin's Glassboro summit meetings, which President Johnson is already beginning to describe as the spirit of Hollybush. If the spirit of Hollybush is the continuation of the journey from the spirit of Camp David, instead of a return to the road which brought the Soviet Union to the pinnacle of power, it would mean the end of the Soviet Union's outstanding authority in international affairs. The near future will show whether Hollybush has been a continuation of the journey from Camp David or is an about-turn in the direction of an uncompromising position on fundamental problems affecting the Third World within the framework of the Soviet Union's ideological responsibilities.

China has now emerged as the undisputed champion of

oppressed peoples and their just causes, and will strive to regain ground lost in Asia and Africa after the failure to hold the Second Afro-Asian Conference and the reverses in Indonesia and Ghana. As a manifestation of the United States' growing influence in the sub-continent, India will find reasons for taking a more conciliatory attitude towards Israel. President Nasser and other Arab leaders will have to subject their policies to extensive reappraisal. They will need to work out priorities, reduce points of conflict, and decide which is the greater threat; Israel or their own inter-Arab rivalries. They will have to review without prejudice the problems of the Yemen and the Persian Gulf, establishing a more durable working arrangement between progressive and conservative regimes. Generally speaking, the United Arab Republic's policies will have to become more inward-looking for some time to come. Most important of all, genuine efforts must be made to bring about a *rapprochement* between Iran and the United Arab Republic.

CHAPTER 10

Relations with Neighbouring Countries and Some Others

Pakistan has established a model relationship with Iran and Turkey, and this fraternal association is an increasingly powerful factor in Asia. The Regional Co-operation for Development, popularly called RCD, will bring our countries closer together as it is based on equality, mutual assistance, and friendship. We should further strengthen our mutual relations and assist one another in overcoming common difficulties by common endeavour.

It is a happy augury for the future that the seemingly intractable prejudices between Turkey and the Arab states are being overcome. Many signs of improvement have recently appeared, but none equalled the encouraging support that Turkey gave the Arab states in their conflict with Israel. Similarly, although relations between Iran and the United Arab Republic have in the past been ruptured, the war in the Middle East and Iran's support for the Arab cause provided an excellent opportunity to repair them. Iraq, Turkey, and Pakistan, all of whom maintain good relations with both Iran and the United Arab Republic, are individually and collectively in a position to assist in the process of restoring normal relations between the two countries. What appeared difficult before the conflict, should now be less difficult after the Iranian demonstration of sympathy with the Arabs. A *rapprochement* between these countries would help greatly in bringing peace to the troubled Middle East and the explosive situation in the Gulf region.

To turn now to the underdeveloped countries of Latin America, it is necessary for Pakistan to maintain good relations with these, both to secure fairer terms of international trade and better economic conditions of co-operation between the developed and underdeveloped nations, and also to foster common political aspirations. Latin America is far away from Pakistan, but distance should not be accepted as an obstacle to the cultivation of good relations. Many of the problems of Latin America are similar to those of Asia and Africa. It would not be difficult to establish friendly relations with the countries of Latin America, provided we continue to associate ourselves with the aspirations of all underdeveloped countries struggling for a better life. The principle of self-determination is sacrosanct to the nations of Latin America. Chiefly for this reason, in spite of Pakistan's limited contacts with that continent, we have been able to surmount the difficulties of distance and have had Latin America's support in the United Nations on Jammu and Kashmir. It is all the more necessary for Pakistan to develop her contacts with the states of Latin America, especially with the important nations of Mexico, Cuba, Brazil, and Argentina.

Being in two parts, Pakistan has more neighbours than many other countries; on the western side, Iran, Afghanistan, China, and the Soviet Union, which is separated from Pakistan by a few miles; on our eastern flank, Burma, and, separated by short distances, Nepal, Bhutan, and Sikkim. The territory of India lies between East and West Pakistan. Because of their position, West Pakistan needs to establish cordial relations with countries as far away as Algeria; and East Pakistan, with countries as far to the east as Indonesia and Japan.

Pakistan's relations with Iran are excellent and there is no reason why our nations cannot continue to consolidate their mutual relations to stabilize peace in our region. Afghanistan, another Muslim state, is a contiguous neighbour of Pakistan, and good relations with that country would be in the interest of both. For reasons of history, faith, and geography, we have more common links with Afghanistan than with any other country in Asia. Ironically, and perhaps on account of their many affinities, on occasions there is a low tide in our relations, but, whatever the ebb and flow of political life, it is essential for two neighbouring Muslim states to maintain fraternal relations. It is possible for us to protect our vital national interests, and yet be on good terms with that country. For obvious reasons, India makes great efforts to win the good graces of Afghanistan.

Nepal is to Pakistan what Afghanistan is to India. Afghanistan is land-locked by Pakistan and is a Muslim monarchy. It has good relations with the Soviet Union and a northern land route crosses its territory. Nepal is land-locked by India and is a Hindu monarchy. It has good relations with China and a road connects them. Nepal's proximity to East Pakistan and to the vital states of Sikkim and Bhutan; and the Province of Assam with its Naga and Mizo freedom fighters, not to speak of up-risings in the Nexalbari corridor, gives Nepal a high place in the calculations of Pakistan's foreign policy. Until a few years back, our relations with Nepal were virtually non-existent. More recently, however, strenuous efforts have been made to make up for lost time, and our relations have improved in all spheres. There are prospects of yet greater collaboration, which will promote increasing understanding between Pakistan and Nepal. Sikkim and Bhutan are also Pakistan's neighbours, but unfor-tunately India does not permit any contacts with these states, which she regards as her feudatories. One day, no doubt, the spirit of independence and national assertion of these northern Himalayan states will break the barriers of isolation and give Pakistan an opportunity to develop relations of mutual benefit with them. Like Jammu and Kashmir, Nepal, Sikkim, and Bhutan are perched on the Himalayan mountain range to form a precious geo-political necklace, the value of which should not be lost in the context of sub-continental politics. This vulnerable region could yet become another Vietnam.

Pakistan should make every endeavour to maintain the most cordial relations with Burma, a state which has a common border with East Pakistan and the troubled regions of India. The boundary with Burma has been demarcated, and our contacts have been developing steadily in all spheres of our bilateral relations. There is peace and undersantding on the Arakan border, which has increased mutual confidence. Indonesia has no common frontier with Pakistan, but its special relations with our country, formed during the era of President Soekarno, qualify it to be regarded as a neighbour in the broader sense of the word. We hope that the changes that have taken place there will not obstruct the further growth of good relations between the two most populous Muslim countries.

Although Pakistan has no common boundary with the Soviet Union, we are close enough to be neighbours. Pakistan–Soviet relations have been marred by a past history for which neither Pakistan nor the Soviet Union is entirely responsible. At the time of Pakistan's Independence, there was every indication that our relations would develop on the basis of reciprocal interests, but later events were to disappoint that expectation. Pakistan became a member of the Defence Alliance at the height of the Soviet–American confrontation and thus incurred the hostility of the Soviet Union, which considered all pacts to be directed against its basic national and international interests. In its anxiety to give constant proof of its fidelity to the United States' global policies, Pakistan followed at times an immoderate line, with the result that the Soviet Union retaliated by supporting India over Jammu and Kashmir. The differences were skilfully exploited by Prime Minister Nehru to worsen the state of Pakistan–Soviet relations. Spurred by the changes in the international situation, a break-through in Pakistan–Soviet relations was achieved when, as Minister for Fuel, Power and Natural Resources, I visited the Soviet Union at the end of 1960 to conclude an Oil Agreement with that country. This was the first contact of major significance between the Soviet Union and Pakistan and it opened the way to contacts in other fields. It is a heartening sign that in recent years Pakistan's relations with the Soviet Union have continued to improve.

China and India are our most important immediate neighbours and will be discussed separately. As regards relations in general, it can be claimed that Pakistan has managed to establish cordial ties with most of its many neighbours. This is no mean achievement.

CHAPTER 11

Pakistan and the Vietnam War

Before discussing Pakistan's relations with China and India, it is necessary to touch upon Vietnam, the most burning issue now facing the world. Like Pakistan, Vietnam has a historical past of subjection to colonial domination. This the Vietnamese people have gallantly resisted from the earliest period. Shortly after the Second World War, they were obliged, when all attempts to come to terms with their former colonial rulers failed, to take up arms against France which was then supported by other Western states. That war of liberation forced the French to leave the country. The Geneva Agreements of 1954 were intended to constitute the framework of a free and independent Vietnam, but the United States intervened and frustrated the objectives of these Agreements.

In the beginning, the United States sent 'advisers' and 'military observers', under the pretext of combating Communism, to assist the South Vietnam regime in the civil war, which it had intensified by its increasing military involvement. In the Spanish Civil War many persons of liberal conviction came from other parts of Europe and the United States to the help of the Republicans. After General Franco's victory, Western Europe and the United States treated Spain for many years as an outcast, ostracizing it from the Western community. How different is the case of Vietnam, where the liberal and progressive forces are being crushed to prevent the country from becoming Communist!

It is a matter of conjecture whether the United States believed, from the beginning, that its commitment in Vietnam would become as extensive as it now is. Pity and justice have been sacrificed to overweening national pride. The United States is probably capable of achieving a military victory in Vietnam, but such a victory would not provide the political answer to a problem which defies all but political solutions.

The United States envisages its future role in Asia as depending on the outcome of the Vietnamese war, and is therefore determined to continue its participation to the bitter end. Already the war is causing stresses in the *détente* between the United States and the Soviet Union. China has not yet committed her armed forces to the struggle, but provocative military actions are nevertheless being taken against Chinese territory, which could lead to an alarming enlargement of the conflict. American troops alone in Vietnam, excluding the personnel of the Seventh Fleet, have exceeded 470,000. The South Vietnam regime and the American Generals are pressing for more troops. General Westmoreland, the United States Army Commander, was summoned to the United States to address Congress with the purpose of mustering more support for the intensification of the war, and returning from his ninth visit to Vietnam, Defence Secretary McNamara stated that more troops were needed for the United States' war effort. On 3 August 1967, President Johnson asked Congress to increase the reinforcements by 'at least 45,000' in the current fiscal year. At the same time he urged Congress to impose a 10 per cent surcharge on individual and corporate income taxes, totalling $6·5 billion, to meet the rising cost of the war in Vietnam. To take such severe measures in a pre-election year only shows the magnitude of the United States' predicament.

Aerial bombardment of North Vietnam has become so ferocious as to amount to a scorched-earth policy. Saturation bombing has been resorted to, employing special fragmentation bombs which release razor-sharp slivers of steel. Napalm and phosphorous bombs containing chemicals which burn fiercely and are practically impossible to extinguish with earth or water, have been dropped both in the North and South. Their victims suffer agonies from the burns inflicted, their flesh rots on their bodies and, if they survive, they are maimed for life. The United States is experimenting with its latest murderous weapons in order to bring the North Vietnamese to the negotiating table before the campaign for the American Presidential Elections of 1968 gains momentum; but escalation has an end point. There remain only three or four major steps and therefore the enlargement of the war cannot be ruled out. It is a terrible gamble to which international opinion and a section of opinion in the United States are opposed. In Europe and in Asia resentment against the United States' military actions is growing proportionately to the intensification of the war. To counter its increasing isolation, the United States seeks the participation of other countries on its side in the war. That is why so much pressure is being brought to bear on Pakistan to make some token contribution to the United States' war effort, but under no circumstances, no matter how heavy the pressure, should we weaken in our resolve to have no part in that war or desist from condemning its continuance. Such a stand might entail the loss of economic and military assistance, but by defending its just position, Pakistan would finally gain much more than it loses in material terms. It is all very well in times of peace to bemoan the loss of material aid, and to envy the numerous benefits of economic and military assistance to countries like Thailand, which, because of its support to the United States, is obtaining aid in colossal quantities. The benefits and risks have to be considered not only in times of peace, but also in terms of the consequences of war, if such assistance is meant to draw the recipient nation into war. At present Thailand's economy may thrive, but if the war spreads to that country, to what extent will Thailand have benefited?

The Vietnamese fight for freedom is an inspiration to all nations exposed to intervention from Great Powers. The sacrifices made by that country may well benefit all underdeveloped nations, but the lesson of Vietnam is not only one of heroism; for it has a darker side. The war could not continue without the corruption of a small number of Vietnamese like the religious fanatic Diem, who hoped to make South Vietnam a separate state by destroying all religions except Christianity. The United States helped him because he conceded to it the right to its physical presence in his country. From this point start the real misfortunes of Vietnam. The war of liberation from the old colonial power was over, but a new war had begun against the intervention of a neo-colonialist power. The memory of the old system is being revived in Vietnam by the privileges accorded to the nationals of a foreign power.

Pakistan must think not only of the immediate gains of economic and military assistance, but of the consequences, if the donor's object is to enlarge the war. Pakistan might itself become a battlefield, and it is absolutely essential that we resist every pressure designed to entangle us in this disastrous conflict. The future of Asia and of the sub-continent will depend on its outcome. It cannot last for ever, but must give way to peace and once this is restored, many far-reaching changes are likely to take place in the interpretation of the United States' global objectives and of its place in Asia. Pakistan must wait patiently for the turn of events.

Diplomacy is a flexible art. What appears to be impossible today is possible tomorrow. If President Kennedy had not been assassinated, the Vietnam war might well have taken a different course. A constructive dialogue might have begun between China and the United States, on the lines of that begun between President Kennedy and Premier Khrushchev in Vienna, which led to the *détente* between the United States and the Soviet Union.

CHAPTER 12

Sino-Pakistani Relations

Pakistan's relations with China have greatly improved since 1962. This has caused misgivings in the United States, where the rationale of this relationship has been much distorted. Sino-Pakistani relations are not primarily based on the differences of the two countries with India. That factor forms only a part, important though it be, of the rationale. China is Pakistan's neighbour and it is essential for us to maintain good relations with all our neighbours on the basis of friendship and equality. There are no territorial or other disputes between the countries to give rise to differences. Ever since the Revolution in China, the leaders of that country have made sincere efforts to establish normal relations with Pakistan. During the Bandung Conference, Premier Chou En-Lai assured the Prime Minister of Pakistan that China desired good relations with Pakistan, and it would have been unwise for Pakistan to have spurned a gesture of goodwill from a powerful neighbouring country. China's dominant place in Asia is assured; Pakistan is an Asian state, whose destinies are forever linked with those of Asia, and it is vital for Pakistan to maintain friendly relations with China for strengthening Asian unity. As members of the community of Asia and Africa, our countries have a common interest in the promotion of Afro-Asian solidarity—a further reason why they must maintain good relations with each other. As underdeveloped countries, China and Pakistan seek to co-operate with other such countries, for obtaining better international trading terms and for a more equitable participation with the developed states in the economic and social advancement of the underdeveloped nations. From the very beginning, China has taken a just position on the partition of Palestine and has supported the Arab cause against Israel. China's support for the Arab nations is in conformity with Pakistan's position, as was conclusively demonstrated by the bold position China took on the side of the Arab states when Israel launched her recent aggression. Like Pakistan and other Afro-Asian states, China has resolutely condemned apartheid and the racial policies of South Africa and Southern Rhodesia. Most important of all, she has unequivocally supported the right of self-determination of the people of Jammu and Kashmir and this, quite apart from other considerations, must influence Pakistan in seeking friendly relations with China.

As an underdeveloped country, Pakistan would like to see the United Nations reformed, so that it would be in a better position to protect the interests of weaker nations, but this is inconceivable without the participation of the People's Republic of China, a Great Power entitled, in its own right, to a place in the Security Council. Instead of the Global Powers trying to promote a dangerous bilateral reduction of the armed forces of India and Pakistan, the United Nations should work for complete and general international disarmament involving the destruction rather than the monopolization of nuclear weapons. If peace can only be assured in a disarmed world, and if it is desirable to encourage genuine efforts for international disarmament, it is imperative to bring about the participation of China in disarmament negotiations. Complete disarmament will remain a distant goal without the co-operation of a nation of 700 million people that possesses a nuclear arsenal. For all these self-evident reasons, Pakistan's friendly relations with China are motivated by positive factors and not passing exigencies affecting another country.

It has been insinuated that the ideologies of Pakistan and China are incompatible and that a friendly working arrangement cannot therefore be sustained between them. It is further argued that Pakistan's friendly relations with China, being of a subjective character, will be unable to withstand the stress of time. These are fallacious arguments. States deal with states, as such, and not with their social systems or ideologies. If such an argument were carried to its logical conclusion, Pakistan should have friendly relations only with Muslim states and isolate itself from the rest of the world. It is a historical fact that Islam, as a political force, has suffered more at the hands of Christian states than of others. It was Christendom that launched crusades against Islam, and it was the Christian nations which held almost all Muslim states under imperial bondage for centuries, destroying their social and moral fibre to such an extent that the world of Islam is still in the process of recovering from the damage inflicted. Professor Arnold Toynbee has said:

> Centuries before Communism was heard of, our ancestors found their bugbear in Islam. As lately as the sixteenth century, Islam inspired the same hysteria in Western hearts as Communism in the twentieth century, and this essentially for the same reasons. Like Communism, Islam was an anti-Western movement which was at the same time a heretical version of a Western faith; and, like Communism, it wielded a sword of the spirit against which there was no defence in material armaments.[1]

It is unlikely that China is going to be responsible for the fall of the Granada of Pakistan or for the wresting of Jerusalem from the Muslim states. Our relations are based on the Bandung principles and on the strict adherence to the concept of non-interference. Nowhere is it mentioned in the scriptures of Islam that fostering friendship with non-Islamic states involves a compromise of identity.

The people of Pakistan were under Western domination for over a century and a half. Nevertheless Pakistan has maintained friendly relations with all Western states and special relations with the United States and Britain. None of these close contacts have contaminated the religious values of the people of Pakistan. Their country has proudly maintained its Islamic character in spite of Western penetration founded on domination and interference. If Pakistan's polity and social structure is firm enough to withstand the onslaught of Western culture and civilization, it can hold its own against any other ideology, especially of a country that has never dominated ours or interfered in its internal affairs. When relations between the United States and the Soviet Union were unfriendly, equally great opposition was offered to the development of friendly relations between Pakistan and the Soviet Union. It is only when relations between the two Super-Powers improved that the objections disappeared. When relations between China and the United States take a more realistic turn, the United States may be less hostile to Pakistan's friendly relations with China. If Pakistan

[1] *Civilization on Trial*, 1948, pp. 21–2.

were now to take provocative steps against China, her position would be the more perilous when relations between China and the United States improve. We would be left to lag behind as we lagged behind India in our endeavours to improve relations with the Soviet Union. If valuable time is lost in this way, irreparable damage is liable to be caused. It is therefore essential that Pakistan continues to develop friendly relations—and resists all attempts to sever those existing—with China, in view of the existing dictates of United States' global policies. Pakistan must determine its foreign policy on the basis of its own enlightened self-interest, uninfluenced by the transient global requirements of the Great Powers.

CHAPTER 13

Relations with European Powers and Great Powers

It remains to be seen which of the three quasi-Great Powers of Western Europe is capable of making the greatest contribution to Pakistan's national cause in the foreseeable future; but on the basis of her present policy, France seems the most likely. Her support for the principle of self-determination, her effort to free herself from the Atlantic hegemony, and her comprehension of Asian problems has resulted in France's good relations with Pakistan.

During the September war of 1965, France gave Pakistan no cause for disappointment. On the contrary, her attitude in the Security Council was most helpful on account of its opposition to sanctions threatened by the other Great Powers. Even during the Consortium crisis of July 1965, France gave Pakistan both economic and political support. Her global policy coincides with our national and international interests, and she has taken careful note of the negative consequences of India's shrinking status under the shadow of hegemony. France believes that India's conflict with China is not conducive to the cause of peace in Asia; values Pakistan as a country that has developed a relationship of trust and understanding with China; and sympathizes with Pakistan's struggle to keep her identity and sovereignty intact.

Pakistan is on friendly terms with the Federal Republic of Germany and has not so far established any contacts with the other Germany; but because of the limitations of German foreign policy, it cannot be asserted to what extent the Federal Republic, despite its accumulating power, will find itself in a position to offer substantial assistance to Pakistan in the event of heavy pressure being exercised on it. Nevertheless, it is important that we continue to develop friendly relations with

K

that country on account of its inherent importance and its capacity to assist Pakistan in the economic field. It cannot, however, for the present at least, be considered a political lever or replace the military equipment denied by the United States.

Britain's influence has diminished in our region and is now overshadowed by the United States'. Because of her dependence on the United States, and because both India and Pakistan are members of the Commonwealth, Britain will continue to maintain a capricious neutrality. On occasions she will try to support Pakistan, and on others India, but more often India than Pakistan. None the less, we should try to maintain friendly relations with Britain, since, as with the Federal Republic of Germany, good relations with Britain carry a number of advantages. That these countries cannot make a positive and meaningful contribution to the solution of our basic problems should not deter us. We have to buy time and hope for change. Even in the present circumstances, there are many advantages in maintaining the best possible relations with both of them. All subsidiary factors should be put into the pool and on a suitable occasion, effectively utilized, and pushed forward.

The theory of causation is as much applicable to foreign affairs as it is to the law of tort. There is an active interrelationship and mutuality of influence in the conduct of state relations. A foreign policy based on recognized universal principles influences other states, while an expedient or opportunist policy adversely affects the image of a state in its relations with other countries. If Pakistan's policies remain consistent and moral, other states are bound to be favourably influenced. By pursuing a pragmatic policy in relations with France, Britain, and the Federal Republic of Germany, congenial conditions can be created for Pakistan to develop cordial relations with the other states of Western Europe. Past links with these and Pakistan's need for economic assistance make such relations especially desirable. These positive factors acquire added impetus from the growing influence of Pakistan in Asia.

Similar arguments apply in respect of the Socialist states of Eastern Europe, with whom Pakistan's growing association could contribute to the creation of a favourable climate in many spheres. In Eastern as in Western Europe, there are certain key states which require our particular attention; the most important being Roumania, a country which has recently come to the fore by pursuing a courageously far-sighted foreign policy. It is equally necessary to pay attention to the industrially advanced countries of Czechoslovakia and Poland, although they share the Soviet Union's apprehensions of what they call the 'revanchist claims' of Germany.

So far as the continent of Europe as a whole is concerned, an extension of co-operation between East and West would be welcomed by Pakistan. The process of inter-European collaboration would be accelerated by Britain's entry into Europe as a European Power and by the removal of the many barriers that still exist between Eastern and Western Europe. When these developments take place, General de Gaulle's 'independent European Europe', a Europe making its own distinct contribution to the preservation of world peace, will be born.

In Pakistan's relations with the United States we have seen the practical manifestation of the policy of imposing rigid preconditions for normal relations. Pakistan was supported in her dispute with India over Jammu and Kashmir because, for certain self-evident reasons, it was in the United States' interest so to support her. Having failed to spread its wings over non-aligned India, the United States turned to Pakistan and, as a consequence, supported us on Jammu and Kashmir on a *quid pro quo* basis. Changes in the international situation have brought about adjustments in the original position of the United States, dictated by global interests and strategy, without bearing either on the merits of the dispute or the reason why we identified our interests with those of that Power.

After the Tibetan crisis and the Sino-Indian border clashes, the United States found fresh opportunities for attracting India to its sphere of influence. Every such contingency is reflected in its attitude to the problem of Jammu and Kashmir. When it was in its global interest to provide military assistance to Pakistan, not all the protestations of Pandit Nehru had any effect on its decision to supply arms to Pakistan. Again, when it was in the United States' interest to supply arms to India, our own protests, violent as they were, had no effect on the United States' policy to provide such arms. In February 1963, the American Government sent Mr. Phillips Talbot, Assistant Secretary of State, on a visit to the sub-continent. He said in Pakistan that, to keep the balance of power in the region, the United States would not give more arms aid to Pakistan; adding that, just as the United States continued to supply arms to Pakistan despite Indian protests in the past, his Government would likewise continue to supply arms to India despite Pakistan's protests. In that respect the United States' policy remained obdurate. The flow of arms increased, as did economic aid and the despatch of food-grains, and the entire scope of support to India multiplied without pause. One can say that aid to India increased in almost geometrical proportion to Pakistan's protestations.

In the case of the Soviet Union, we find that its traditional policy of complete identification with non-aligned India over Jammu and Kashmir has undergone some alteration on account of changes in the global situation. The state of our relations had little influence in bringing about adjustments in the Soviet Union's attitude when those adjustments were required by its global interests. They were carried out in spite of India's protestations. The Soviet Union chose to ignore Pakistan's membership of military alliances and the U-2 flights when it served its global interests to make some adjustments to its attitude over Jammu and Kashmir in order to contain China. Likewise, when relations between India and China were cordial and relations between Pakistan and China were not, China refused for its own reasons to support India on the issue of Jammu and Kashmir. When Prime Minister Nehru failed to get China's support, he sought to associate China with India symbolically by pressing Prime Minister Chou En-Lai to visit Srinagar during his visit to India. Although relations between Pakistan and China were far from normal in those days, the Chinese Prime Minister, keeping an eye on the future, flatly refused to allow himself to be drawn into even a symbolic support of India.

During the September war of 1965, all the Great Powers took their stance according to their respective global evaluation of the war. The United States was under a treaty obligation to assist Pakistan but, instead of rendering assistance, it cut off all military aid to Pakistan and imposed an economic embargo on its SEATO and CENTO partner. The Soviet Union, alarmed by the Chinese ultimatum and fearing one more serious political and ideological cleavage with China, sought sedulously to end the conflict. So great was its concern to terminate hostilities that, for the second time only in its history as a socialist state, it offered its good offices, this time for the resolution of Indo-Pakistan disputes. China's open support for Pakistan, in spite of the sound political reasons for it, was unprecedented. The positions taken by the three Global Powers were determined not by their treaty relations nor by the extent of India's or Pakistan's identification with them, but by their global aims.

Pakistan has not succeeded in converting the United States to its point of view through bilateral or multilateral means, including complete identification with its interests. India and the United States are now on better terms, but even when relations between the two countries were strained and there were no differences between Pakistan and the United States, Pakistan could not persuade the United States to use its influence with India to resolve her disputes with us. The United States hesitated to exert its influence on India in favour of aligned and friendly Pakistan, even though it was in a position to do so. No earnest attempt was made to promote an equitable settlement. In a White House briefing in May 1962, President Kennedy observed that 'Pakistan's request for help in Kashmir involving India demonstrates an effort to borrow the United States power for other nationalistic purposes.' Pakistan was then not only seeking American intervention, but was imposing a condition on the United States to settle the Jammu and Kashmir dispute in order to have normal relations. By persistently taking this dangerous course, we came close to enforcing—albeit inadvertently—an unfair settlement.

How then should Pakistan protect her interests and maintain cordial relations with the United States? A complete answer is difficult to find, but a relatively safe solution is obvious enough: by rejecting preconditions for normal relations and making it clear that interference in our national objectives will not be tolerated. We should seek to put in quarantine the points of disagreement and develop relations in areas of common understanding. If, despite such an approach, the United States were to persist in seeking to bring about a settlement not based on self-determination, and in seeking Indo-Pakistani co-operation for its global political purposes, Pakistan should be prepared for a diplomatic confrontation which in time would have to give way to normal relations based on a new under-standing. It is better to take a stand and face a period of difficulty than to yield to pressure, open the floodgates, and admit one crisis after another. By arriving at a new arrange-ment in which the United States' 'power would not be bor-rowed', to use the words of President Kennedy, we would be unburdening that country of an embarrassing responsibility and simultaneously protecting our vital national interests. By insulating the points of difference, we would in no way forfeit our right to pursue our causes vigorously, and other means are available to press forward our claims, perhaps with greater chances of success. Rather than perpetuate a demoralizing stale-mate with a Great Power, it is wiser to cut the knot that has become a noose. Yugoslavia has not supported Pakistan's posi-tion on Jammu and Kashmir; nevertheless, our relations with that country are cordial. This is because we have developed relations with Yugoslavia in areas of agreement and have not sought that country's intervention for the resolution of our disputes with India. We have inadvertently insulated the point of difference with that country in our mutual relations and have thus avoided diplomatic strains. We can continue to demonstrate our desire for support and make indirect efforts to obtain it, yet maintain normal relations outside the ambit of the differences while they last.

We should thus make it clear to every Great and Global Power that Pakistan is prepared for normal relations with each of them separately, on a bilateral basis outside the realm of currently irreconcilable differences, provided that the Power in each case desists from interfering in the country's affairs against the country's interest. We would maintain normal but qualified relations without preconditions in exchange for non-interference in our internal affairs, in our struggle for the libera-tion of the people of Jammu and Kashmir, and in the equitable resolution of other disputes with India. Such an approach would be consistent, logical, and, in the long run, the least obstructive to the attainment of our objectives. It would provide us with an opportunity for normal relations with all states, yet be reconcilable with the active pursuit of our objectives. It would give us freedom to pursue our legitimate objectives with-out fear of inimical foreign intervention, and would not prevent us from endeavouring by indirect influences and persuasion to bring about favourable changes in the attitude of those Powers which are either hostile or neutral. There is a fundamental difference between 'preconditions for normal relations' and 'persuasion' without preconditions. By not seeking intervention for the resolution of our disputes, we would not be prevented from trying to persuade other countries to take a right position. It goes without saying that, if a state were to change its position voluntarily on account of the application of indirect pressure, or for other reasons, there would be a corresponding change in our bilateral relations with that state.

We must recognize clearly that no Global Power can, through its diplomatic support, effect the hand-over of Jammu and Kashmir to Pakistan. At the same time, their active political opposition can make it more difficult for us to achieve our aims. We should therefore seek to disengage those states that are either neutral or opposed to our position, by setting the points of difference outside the range of our bilateral relations. Conversely, we should consolidate our relations with all those countries, especially the Great and Global Powers, which give Pakistan unqualified support over the Jammu and Kashmir dispute. No country would have reason to take exception to priorities established on a clear and rational basis of supreme national interest without preconditions. It would be understood that the whole basis of Pakistan's foreign policy was to consolidate relations with those who support us in our just causes, and to insulate the points of conflict with those Great and Global Powers that are opposed to our just struggle. Our cordial relations with countries supporting us would not be ascribable to ulterior motives and would demonstrate that we are not pawns in any global contest, but that there is a perfect explanation for a gradation in the relations with all countries. In this way, we would put our relations with the three Global Powers on a rational basis without preconditions, relatively consistent with their interests, in complete accord with our own, and without fear of interference.

To be more specific, it would be advisable for Pakistan to avoid a direct confrontation with the Global Powers over disputes with India. We should not seek to lay down conditions with them for normal relations. We should be prepared to have cordial but qualified relations with those that are either opposed or neutral with regard to our position; qualified, because of their different positions on disputes of fundamental importance to our nation, but without strain, as we would differ and yet maintain normal relations without fear of intervention. Our interests will be less well served by unprofitable debates than by our creating conditions such as would influence the Great Powers to change their position on account of objective compulsions. This is a difficult undertaking, but it can be achieved by unifying the support we have from those Great and Global Powers as are unequivocally in favour of our just cause with that expressed by the underdeveloped nations of Asia, Africa, and Latin America. All will depend on our strategy and resolve.

Let us consider the opposite position. Were we to insist that the Great and Global Powers should support us in our differences with India, before we proceed to have normal relations with them, we would leave them with no choice but to interfere in our internal affairs and impose unfavourable settlements on us, in order to establish normal relations. Such preconditions would be injurious to our vital interests, result in a series of intolerable compromises, and introduce double dealings in our relations with all Great and Global Powers.

Our own effort is of primary importance in the attainment of our higher objectives, yet we are not likely to succeed by these alone. We require international support, some of which we already receive from the majority of the smaller states committed to decolonization and self-determination. We have the support of one Great Power in Asia and are in a position to obtain the same from at least one quasi-Great Power in Europe. If, backed by such powerful collective support, we proceed to act correctly and with discretion, we should be able to exercise much influence on other states, both great and small, in the realization of our just claims. We would free ourselves from entanglements and thereby avoid being exposed to moral, material, and diplomatic pressures. Having reached a position of relative safety we should wait for the favourable moment, which the complex international situation is more than likely to furnish. Until then, by hindering the pressure of interference, we would escape the imposition of an unfavourable settlement on Jammu and Kashmir and bring consistency in our bilateral relations with all states.

Global Power policies do undergo adjustments. The dynamics of the world situation require that the smaller nations should seek to isolate areas of conflict with Global Powers in the pursuit of their individual, in contrast to their collective, objectives. Twenty years is not a long time in the life of a nation, and we should continue with determination to uphold our just cause. We cannot forsake a moral, ideological obligation only because the odds appear at present to be against us. The people of Vietnam have faced destruction for over twenty years. Though their villages and cities are being razed to the ground, their spirit of resistance is firmer than ever. It is better to have a stalemate and no solution at all than to agree to an unjust solution. An ignominious compromise would reduce the chances of a just settlement in the future.

Pakistan's immediate task is to reduce and if possible eliminate foreign interference, which is growing at a menacing pace and which, if not arrested, could not only lead to an unjust settlement of the Jammu and Kashmir dispute, but also involve us in an anti-China axis in collaboration with India. Therefore a change is called for in the traditional diplomatic approach. Quite against the spirit of our times, against the spirit of Bandung too, we have, to our peril, encouraged foreign interference and intervention. Foreign powers would not seek to resolve our disputes if the solutions work against their interest. Once the foreign influence is eliminated, it should be possible to look anew at problems in their proper perspective. The proposition reduced to its simplest form amounts to this, that under no circumstances must Pakistan get entangled in the ideological or territorial disputes of the Global Powers. We must maintain a non-committal attitude in global confrontations, but, at the same time, take a clear and independent position on world issues affecting the rights of peoples and nations to equality, self-determination, and economic emancipation. Uninfluenced by the attitude of other nations, Pakistan must always oppose aggression and stand behind the victims, in conformity with the noblest norms of its ideology. We should demonstrate strict neutrality in the ideological confrontation of the Global Powers. In determining her relations with such Powers, Pakistan must also take into account her geographical situation and the support she receives in her own just causes. She must formulate her policies on the merits of each case, without taking a predetermined position in the global rivalries. These policies must be in accordance with the concept of non-interference in the internal affairs of a country and self-determination for all nations. She must refrain from accepting preconditions which limit her freedom of action in any respect in the discharge of her national and ideological obligations.

CHAPTER 14

Some Conclusions

In view of past experience and other considerations Pakistan must pursue three principal objectives:

1. A policy of friendship and good faith with China, a Great Power with whom its basic interests conform.
2. Good relations with the United States and the Soviet Union, but without preconditions and on the basis of non-interference; also with the nations of Eastern and Western Europe, especially France, Germany, Britain, Roumania, Czechoslovakia, and Poland.
3. The strengthening of the Third World—the under-developed nations of Latin America, Asia, and Africa, and, in particular, Muslim nations and neighbouring countries.

The realization of these objectives would secure, so to speak, Pakistan's flanks and rear, enabling us to face the rising tide of difficulties with India, which has become more acute on account of the changes in American sub-continental policies. If Pakistan is not prepared to resist these, she should, at least, take an unambiguous stand as did Burma and Cambodia some time ago. One sharp and decisive encounter at the political level would put a stop to the downward trend, and is infinitely preferable to a step-by-step retreat ending perhaps in dismemberment. In international politics, ready prescriptions are not available as they are in medicine, but this does not mean that remedies are not available for political ailments.

The United States' decision to terminate military assistance to Pakistan and its general policies in the sub-continent have considerably increased the threat to Pakistan's security. We must therefore take remedial measures, and the sooner the better for peace in the sub-continent. India's armed strength is greater than Pakistan's. The United States' decision and

increasing support for India calls for positive measures to safeguard Pakistan's position and, in particular, to maintain a
military balance with India.

The United States has arbitrarily and without notice abrogated the letter and spirit of the Mutual Defence Treaties and
CENTO and SEATO Agreements. Solemn commitments to
Pakistan have not been honoured. In Vietnam, on the other
hand, the world is being taken towards an international catastrophe in the name of commitments. As the United States has
unilaterally broken its agreements with Pakistan, these agreements are no longer valid. From the date of the announcement
of cessation of military assistance to Pakistan, all defence agreements with the United States have become null and void. As
these have lapsed, Pakistan should ask the United States to
close the remaining special facilities granted to it on Pakistan
territory and withdraw its personnel from the bases, along with
the remaining MAAG personnel, on 1 July 1967, as announced
by Washington. If these facilities are terminated immediately,
it would be a timely mark of our good intentions towards the
Soviet Union and China. Even a delay in closing down the
American Communications Centre at Peshawar might prove
counter-productive. If Pakistan's corrective actions do not
closely follow the stoppage of military assistance, the United
States might not construe them to be of a reciprocal character.
In that event new complications will unnecessarily arise in our
mutual relations and in Pakistan's efforts to redress the balance
from other quarters.

If, however, Pakistan allows the agreements which have
already been broken, to come to their stipulated conclusion, it
would mean assuming a perilous unilateral commitment to the
United States without any corresponding obligation. It is
simple common sense that, in the discharge of an elementary
obligation to the people of Pakistan, the Government should
declare the Mutual Defence Agreements and the pacts to have
become non-existent, and formally withdraw from CENTO and
SEATO. It was certainly unwise to have participated in the last
SEATO Ministerial Conference in Washington, in April 1967.
If, however, participation was considered necessary, a powerful
delegation should have been sent to expose the real reasons for
the United States' decision. Before leaving SEATO altogether,

Pakistan should have made clear to that meeting and to the people of the United States the grave situation in Asia and the terrible consequences of escalating the Vietnam war. By expressing the anguish of the Asian peoples, Pakistan would have earned international respect and strengthened the position taken by France. It might have encouraged the United Kingdom to take the position she would like to adopt. Pakistan should have led the movement for peace in Asia on the soil of the United States, where a large and increasing section of public opinion, including prominent leaders of both parties, are incensed over the war. Our voice would have represented not only the people of Asia, but humanity everywhere. Pakistan should have made it clear that she was being penalized not because of the Indo-Pakistani impasse, but primarily because she refused to soil her hands by participation in the Vietnam war. Having taken an unassailable position in the Conference, Pakistan would have served the interest of world peace, and world opinion would have been sympathetic. Such a position would have created a propitious political climate for future negotiations with the Soviet Union, China, France, and other countries. It appears, however, that it was decided at the Guam Conference, and in subsequent meetings, to prepare for further escalation of the Vietnam war in order to achieve a military victory. The sooner, therefore, that Pakistan dissociates herself from treaties which are no longer valid, the better for her future security and for peace in Asia. We cannot permit treaties which no longer offer security to us, but actively threaten our security, to be used as springboards for the escalation of the Vietnam war.

It is not by any means fortuitous that almost all countries which have received military assistance from the United States have, in one way or the other, been involved in internal troubles or in conflicts with Communist Powers. South Korea has endured a war; the off-shore islands of China have been shelled; the Philippines, Thailand, and Japan have had grave external and internal problems. Greece has been through an internal conflict, which continues under the surface; and after the Second World War, there was trouble on the northern borders of Iran. Pakistan is among the fortunate few to have escaped such troubles, but this situation cannot last for ever and it would be an act of wisdom to leave SEATO and CENTO immediately. At the 1967 SEATO Conference in Washington, the Foreign Minister of Thailand is reported to have remarked that 'it is a harrowing situation that there could be some who seek to derive only advantages from membership of SEATO without accepting the corresponding obligations and responsibilities, at this grave juncture while many of our youth are risking their lives and a number of them fallen in the battlefield fighting for a lofty cause'. It is further reported that he could not see how, under such circumstances, SEATO 'based on unequal rights and obligations can adequately continue to function'. He thought that SEATO 'will go through the inevitable process of evolution and seek to adjust itself on a basis of more corresponding mutuality of interest'. With such remarks emanating from a Member State of SEATO, and with the announcement of Britain's latest White Paper on defence that obligations to SEATO will be 'progressively altered in nature and size', it would be better if Pakistan took the initiative to leave the pacts before she finds herself facing greater difficulties.

Despite the aligned nature of Pakistan's foreign policy and the fact of receiving military assistance to combat Communism, we have been spared conflicts with Communist states on account of objective common interests with the People's Republic of China in Asia and in the sub-continent. India is an adversary of Pakistan and has a dispute with China. China seems to be of the opinion that India will become increasingly dependent on the United States and gradually, under its influence, adopt a position hostile to China. For this reason, it is in China's national interest to support Pakistan and it is in Pakistan's national interest to develop friendly relations with China. Of all the countries which have received military assistance from the United States to combat Communism, Pakistan alone has a fundamental common interest with one of the most powerful Communist states. This is a unique position, a freak in the global permutations.

As Pakistan has no quarrel with the Soviet Union and the People's Republic of China, we should, in view of the latest developments, conclude treaties of friendship and non-aggression with them as soon as possible. We might also consider concluding similar treaties with other Great Powers, although, from a practical point of view, these are unnecessary. There is little use in claiming to be on friendly terms with all countries, whilst remaining members of defence pacts and providing facilities to one Global Power which the others consider to be directed against them. This is a basic contradiction and we should make our relations genuinely non-contradictory.

Pakistan should also consider concluding treaties of friendship and non-aggression with as many of her neighbours as possible. There should be no difficulty in concluding such treaties with Iran, Burma, and Nepal. In addition to a treaty with Nepal, it should be possible to hold constructive discussions on certain other matters of common interest, which would in no way involve that friendly country in our disputes with India. Pakistan should also try to conclude a treaty of friendship and non-aggression with Afghanistan. The present crisis calls for a series of swift diplomatic initiatives. Only by taking them can the anomalies created by the turn in Pakistan's relations with the United States be rectified.

The United States exercises considerable influence in Western Europe. It would therefore be difficult for Pakistan to succeed in making the NATO powers deviate from the basic American attitude to the supply of military equipment. Nevertheless, efforts should be made to find out to what extent some of them would be willing to co-operate. From Pakistan's point of view, France is by far the most important country in Western Europe, and it is questionable whether France would be influenced by the United States' recent decisions. The sooner we develop a special understanding with that country the better for us both.

CHAPTER 15

The State's Best Defence

The Pakistan Government will have to undertake measures to make the country's economic and food resources self-supporting. Most underdeveloped countries need foreign assistance and ours is no exception. Foreign assistance should serve to turn a dependent economy into a self-reliant one, but, if it is accompanied by foreign interference, dependence increases and the object is defeated. It has yet to be seen whether the economies of India and Pakistan have moved towards self-reliance at all with the heavy foreign investments on the Western pattern in the last decade or so. There are conflicting opinions on the growth of Pakistan's economy. Some are of the view that Pakistan has made tremendous strides and become a model Asian State, second only to Japan! Others maintain that Pakistan's economic development has been erratic, irrational, and not in accord with its resources and essential needs. There are signs of growth and development and there are also indications of serious economic trouble. With sustained effort and with a change in the economic system, Pakistan can overcome her economic difficulties. The country's Achilles' heel is her food-grain deficit of 2·5 million tons, but, with this problem solved, she would be in a position to withstand a multitude of international pressures. Unfortunately, much precious time has been lost. If the Government of Pakistan had paid as much attention to agriculture in its Second Five Year Plan as it is doing in the current Plan, the country would have become self-sufficient by now. But the policy of the Second Five Year Plan was irrationally directed to industrial development in all fields except that of the basic industries. It was then argued that Pakistan was too poor to afford heavy industries such as the production of steel, and that the country should not strive to attain self-sufficiency in agriculture, because its food deficit could always be met by generous assistance from the United

States under PL-480. This was the work of a Finance Minister who was simultaneously an Executive Director of the World Bank. His policies brought the country to the brink of economic catastrophe. A new class of capitalist baron, as rapacious as any in Latin America, was created to control the national wealth. The system adopted was anything but *laissez faire*. Businessmen, under government patronage, were given licences that converted the collective resources of the nation into personal fortunes. Predatory capitalism ran riot with all the inevitable political consequences, and the country became more rather than less dependent on foreign assistance. That is now a thing of the past; Pakistan today has no other alternative but to make a revolutionary break-through in agriculture and become self-sufficient.

The United States has shown its hand. Great Power actions are systematic and sustained, and Pakistan should now be prepared to face a variety of interconnected pressures, overt and concealed. The coming years are going to be of crucial importance. Following the termination of military assistance, the United States will try to bring matters to a head in the sub-continent, provided the situation in Vietnam permits. Pakistan might have to counter further pressures on her economy and essential supplies. Already a decline in the economic buoyancy is evident. The foreign exchange position has become unsatisfactory, and the drain on our meagre reserves is likely to increase with the repayment of foreign debts and in meeting the country's growing economic, military, and food requirements. As it is, approximately $90 million were spent last year on the import of food-grains. With the stoppage of military assistance and the enforcement of stringent conditions for the supply of spare parts, the Government would be called upon to meet the country's new and additional defence requirements by utilizing its own foreign exchange. The price of jute, Pakistan's main foreign exchange earner, has fallen sharply. The closure of the Suez Canal for an uncertain period will not only raise freight and insurance rates, but also cause delays in the import of industrial goods and food-grains. This in turn, will influence prices of essential commodities. It is doubtful whether the present agricultural yield is capable of wiping out a substantial part of the 2·5 million ton deficit. The United States' attitude to demands for food-grains would be some index of its thinking.

L

CHAPTER 16

Deterrent against Aggression

Pakistan's security and territorial integrity are more important than economic development. Although such development and self-reliance contribute to the strengthening of the nation's defence capability, the defence requirements of her sovereignty have to be met first. Pakistan will have to pay equal attention to the attainment of self-reliance through economic development and to her defence requirements. A non-industrialized country, without even the basis of a heavy industry, cannot depend entirely on the traditional defence system of a small, though highly efficient, armed force equipped with conventional weapons. The country being poor, the size of the armed forces cannot be large, nor can it be expanded beyond a certain limit; and it is doubtful whether that limit, even if reached, would be high enough should Pakistan be again confronted with an aggressor many times larger, stronger, and better equipped, not to speak of the numerical strength of its armed forces. The economic strain created by the expansion of a standing force would be great, and it would be unwise to think in terms of competing with India in size of forces and quantity of equipment. Pakistan has so far been unable to establish an industrial war-base, for a number of regrettable reasons: one of them being the greed of those for whom the import of steel was more profitable than the production of steel in their own land. It is not possible for Pakistan, within the next few years, to develop a local industrial potential for equipping its armed forces with the more sophisticated weapons; nor can we depend entirely upon ingenious diplomatic initiatives. Indeed, the effect of a nation's diplomatic activities is often related to the weight of its fighting capacity. Many clever things may be said and done, but in the face of real danger a country has to depend on its own strength. International circumstances will change. Therefore, too much reliance upon diplomatic support, without sufficient backing of national security measures, cannot be considered safe. Again, there are set limits to diplomacy on account of certain deficiencies in the structure of Pakistan's economic and political organization. It must be made clear that aggression against Pakistan is a very dangerous affair for the aggressor, and we have this means to find an effective deterrent.

All wars of our age have become total wars; all European strategy is based on the concept of total war; and it will have to be assumed that a war waged against Pakistan is capable of becoming a total war. It would be dangerous to plan for less and our plans should, therefore, include the nuclear deterrent. Difficult though this is to employ, it is vital for Pakistan to give the greatest possible attention to nuclear technology, rather than allow herself to be deceived by an international treaty limiting this deterrent to the present nuclear Powers. India is unlikely to concede nuclear monopoly to others and, judging from her own nuclear programme and her diplomatic activities, especially at Geneva, it appears that she is determined to proceed with her plans to detonate a nuclear bomb. If Pakistan restricts or suspends her nuclear programme, it would not only enable India to blackmail Pakistan with her nuclear advantage, but would impose a crippling limitation on the development of Pakistan's science and technology.

We are, however, not immediately concerned with the question of a nuclear stalemate. Our problem, in its essence, is how to obtain such a weapon in time before the crisis begins. India, whose progress in nuclear technology is sufficient to make her a nuclear Power in the near future, can provoke this at a time of her own choosing. She has already received foreign assistance for her nuclear programme and will continue to receive it. Pakistan must therefore embark on a similar programme, although a nuclear weapon will be neither a real deterrent nor can it be produced in a few years. We must therefore write it off as a practical deterrent in any conflict with India in the near future.

The Vietnam war has proved that a small poor nation can fight the most powerful nation in the world despite its inferiority in technique, wealth, and numbers. Admittedly, the terrain of Vietnam aids the defenders, but there are other overwhelming factors which more than neutralize this advantage. For us the lesson of that war is that a people armed can resist any aggressor; for the Great Powers the lesson is not to get bogged down in such a quagmire. Pakistan's best deterrent would be a national militia, trained and led by professional officers, to support the standing forces in the event of total war. Military training in the universities should be obligatory; in every village there should be created a cadre of active and courageous young men well trained in the use of the primary weapons. In Switzerland every household has to maintain a firearm in good order. The people must defend themselves, and the prospect of a whole nation armed and trained is as powerful a deterrent as an underdeveloped country can hope to possess. The age of gunboat diplomacy has not yet passed away, but not even Global Power military blackmail can be effective when the existence is known of a force determined to resist intervention throughout the whole extent of the territory. Even if the heavy weapons of the regular forces were destroyed by an aggressor's concentrated attacks, there would still remain the resolute fighting units of an armed people. Diffused warfare is extremely costly for the aggressor and offers no hope of a speedy victory. A victory in the old military sense cannot be won against a nation fully armed. Devastation may be achieved, but not victory, and the aggressor, however powerful, must eventually retire disgraced and weakened. Such is the lesson of Vietnam. The knowledge that an attack upon Pakistan would lead to total warfare against a fully armed nation can be the only real deterrent for a relatively more powerful aggressor. Such a deterrent, moreover, would have a strong political value and would give our diplomacy scope for manœuvres more extensive than have hitherto been possible.

This proposal may be objected to on the ground that such a widespread distribution of weapons would increase crime, but the incidence of crime has increased alarmingly over the years, proving that the criminal elements already have the arms. It is the innocent victims of crime who are left defenceless. The fault lies not with the people or with the proposal, but with the social conditions which require radical alteration. If the Government undertakes corrective measures and explains the need to arm the people for self-defence, and if the people are given adequate safeguards, the crime rate will fall and the innocent will be protected, as will every inch of national territory. The distribution of weapons should, of course, be made with discretion and the disciplined militia spread out over the country, rather than concentrated in a few places. Every militiaman's name would be known and criminal elements would not be recruited. In fact, practice in the use of firearms and close-combat methods would assist the people of Pakistan against unruly individuals to whom even the middle class is today hopelessly exposed. The formation of a well-organized and well-supervised militia can only contribute to the maintenance of law and order, by inculcating civic sense.

CHAPTER 17

How to Face the Looming Crisis

A national crisis is a call to national greatness, and must be met with a spirit of dedication. Muslims cannot be better inspired to face such a challenge than by heeding the words of the Holy Koran:

> Fighting in defence of Truth and Right is not to be undertaken light-heartedly, not to be evaded as a duty. Life and Death are in the hands of God. Not all can be chosen to fight for God. It requires constancy, firmness and faith. Given these, large armies can be routed by those who battle for God.

At the time of the Consortium crisis in July 1965, the Government took the issue directly to the people of Pakistan and, with their support, the country successfully surmounted that crisis. The current crisis is more serious and the people must be told the truth: what is wanted of Pakistan and why Pakistan is not in a position to oblige. Underdeveloped countries cannot, by material means, resist the pressures of Great and Global Powers, which can cause havoc by silent diplomacy. They have only to bring into operation a host of devices which wreck the economic and social equilibrium of dependent states and overthrow regimes. Great and Global Powers prefer to operate in silence behind the scenes, and a variety of reasons would be given why discussions on the differences should not be made public. The dependent state would be told that exposure and agitation would further vitiate the atmosphere of the talks. Such states, however, lacking levers to operate directly against Global Powers, have no choice but to expose these machinations and mobilize their people to offer resistance. For this reason, underdeveloped nations seek international platforms like the General Assembly of the United Nations to inform the world of the difficulties involved in their struggle for emancipation and a better life.

It would be a fatal mistake for Pakistan to believe that her existing differences with the United States can be resolved by secret diplomacy and by keeping her people uninformed. These differences and the fundamental problems they raise effect the people's future and must be explained to them. If they have faith in their leaders and confidence in their judgement they would welcome resistance and sacrifice and would stand behind the Government as an invincible force to overcome all national difficulties. The Deputy Chairman of the Planning Commission has said that we are making efforts to diversify our economic dependence. Diversification began about three years ago. It should have taken place earlier, but we were then living in the illusion that, by some minor adjustments, resulting in greater dependency Pakistan would be able to overcome her external difficulties. Pakistan might now lose its final opportunity if we continue to indulge in reveries.

The course of history cannot be changed. We live in Asia and have to take into account the Asian situation, which in less than ten years is likely to undergo revolutionary changes. If we hold firm and take unhesitating steps in the right direction, the crisis will be resolved. There will, of course, be new problems, many appearing insurmountable, but with unity of purpose, there is none that cannot be resolved. The poor people of Pakistan have always risen to the occasion unhesitatingly; now the privileged class must do the same. We cannot escape the responsibilities of leadership. It is for the leaders to hold high the banner of independence and march forward with confidence in a spirit of dedication. Our choice is whether to face the struggle or succumb to external pressures and become a tombstone of the cold war. It is written in the Holy Koran:

And we shall give the joys of victory to those who are oppressed, and who struggle to uphold justice and freedom on the face of the earth; it is they whom we shall raise to be leaders, and it is they who shall be the heirs who shall build up and develop the equal well-being of Man.

The writing on the wall became clear beyond doubt in 1964, when the United States decided to give long-term military assistance to India despite earlier decisions, made in deference to Pakistani fears, to provide India with *ad hoc* assistance subject to review. In taking this new decision the United States took the risk of further straining relations with its most committed Asian ally. When Pakistan swallowed this unpalatable decision and chose not to shirk her cold war commitments in the interests of her own security, the United States concluded that she would not take any counter-measures and accordingly accelerated the rate of aid to India. Pakistan has lost many excellent opportunities to redress her position, and the time for action is slipping past. Timing and initiative, essential ingredients of successful political action, have been as little evidenced in her policies as sound political judgement.

If Pakistan is not prepared to endure sacrifices in overcoming her present difficulties, she will have to come to terms with the United States by co-operating with India by freezing the Kashmir dispute and assuming a different attitude to the People's Republic of China. In return, she would qualify for . United States' military assistance and increased economic aid. The food problem would no longer haunt us. The acceptance of such terms, however, would result in the surrender of vital national interests and, moreover, incur the permanent animosity of China. Pakistan would be condemned without any corresponding benefit; it would lead to greater frustration and result in our encirclement. This would encourage further aggression from India, who seeks joint economic ventures or other concessions only to obtain Pakistan's complete subordination. If relations do not improve with Afghanistan, it would give that country some openings as well. In the event of aggression from India and trouble from Afghanistan, the United States will not assist Pakistan because both are non-Communist countries. The Indo-Pakistan war of 1965 was sufficient proof of the United States' attitude on this point. Conversely, in the event of conflict with China or the Soviet Union, American military assistance would not be sufficient to prevent Pakistan from ultimate defeat.

From every consideration, the only correct course is to establish normal relations with these three Global Powers and to work for the further improvement of relations with all Powers with whom we have a common interest. Three years ago I said, in the National Assembly of Pakistan, that our relations with the United States were abnormal and those with China and the Soviet Union were sub-normal. Our policy should be to normalize relations with all the three Great Powers. We knew that in the interim period there would be difficulties, but we were confident that once the process of normalization was completed, our relations with all three would become cordial.

Pakistan wants to have friendly and normal relations with the United States, a Global Power that has contributed considerably to Pakistan's development. When displeasure with India brought the United States closer to Pakistan, we came to the hasty conclusion that it was our permanent, natural friend; but in international politics the phrase 'natural friend' has no meaning. Its use betrays a romantic outlook on world affairs. Common interest between states exists, but no permanent, natural friendship. The Nehru days are over; India is no longer recalcitrant; and the Indo-Pakistani situation has entered a new phase. It is now in the global interest of the United States to bring Pakistan and India to terms so as to complete the encirclement of China from Japan to the sub-continent. The opportunity exists and the United States will do everything in its power to seize it. After the changes in the Middle East, the American Government might consider that the achievement of its objective in the sub-continent has been considerably facilitated. For a long time Pakistan was not on cordial terms with the two Global Powers who are its immediate neighbours and that was without a conflict of interest with them. Now there is a difference with another Global Power and Pakistan should face it bravely. It has been said by a spokesman of the Foreign Office that a chapter in Pakistan–United States relations has come to an end. I would say that it is more than a chapter. I would say a whole book has been written and it is now on the shelf of history. Let us write the first pages of a new book on the basis of equality and friendship and without false assumptions and without interference in each other's internal affairs. There should be no rancour in our relations. We have helped one another in the past. It cannot be said that Pakistan has not exposed herself to enormous risks and some suffering for the sake of the global policies of the United States, but Pakistan has also derived some advantage from the association and we can still be of service to one another in another context. In inter-state relations the Rubicon is never crossed. In time the hankering after a special relationship will abate, enabling the two countries to co-operate on a more realistic plane where false assumptions, interference, and intervention have no place. Should the United States really desire peace with justice in the conflicts in which it is involved, Pakistan might have an opportunity to lend its efforts. Our relations with the United States have suffered partly because we refused to enlarge the Vietnam war by bearing arms on their side. A time may come when the United States wishes to leave the battlefield in search of peace and Pakistan might then have a notable contribution to make.

Disputes between China and the United States cannot last for ever. Either they will lead to the total destruction of Asia and perhaps countries beyond, or they will subside. If the latter, both will value Pakistan's resistance to Great Power pressure. What appears today to the United States to be an unfriendly attitude might tomorrow appear to be in the interest of lasting peace and, thus, in the higher interests of the United States itself. If our cause is just we can face any situation, even, if need be, complete isolation—though a just cause is seldom isolated.

Pakistan should strive to avoid a political confrontation with the United States over its disputes with India, but it should not shrink from this if, in spite of everything, the United States continues to pursue a policy directed against our interests. We should attempt to disengage the United States in our disputes with India and establish normal relations with it, unqualified by preconditions, on the understanding that it would not interfere in our internal affairs and coerce Pakistan to come to a settlement with India prejudicial to Pakistan's vital interests. If such an attempt fails, it would be preferable to pursue a policy of collective confrontation with the support of the countries of the Third World, most of which support Pakistan on the issue of self-determination, and with that of those Great and quasi-Great Powers which are in sympathy with us.

In late 1958 and early 1959 unsuccessful efforts were made to persuade India and Pakistan to co-operate in defence. One of the main reasons for the failure of that plan was that the ground was insufficiently prepared in advance by the United States. Circumspect efforts are now being made in the light of past experience. There is talk of an exchange of visits between the leaders and journalists, and of a relaxation of travel restrictions between the two countries. At the same time emphasis is placed on the need for joint projects and the reduction of armed forces. The idea is to stabilize the *status quo* and to sanctify it one day by an accord, or a series of minor accords, ending with the final solution.

CHAPTER 18

The Origins of Dispute with India

Relations between India and Pakistan should resemble those between Sweden and Norway, countries which had to break apart in order to come closer to each other. India and Pakistan have so much in common that the rest of the world sometimes finds it hard to understand why they are in a state of perpetual confrontation. The dictates of reason, the compulsions of geography, and the influence of international forces require them to live in peace, but their poverty-stricken masses have been denied the benefits that ought to have accrued to them from political independence. There are many reasons for this state of affairs: the legacy of history, superstition, and prejudice. The Hindus of the sub-continent have borne a thousand years of subjugation and the Muslims have been victims of foreign domination for over 150 years. The mental outlook of all peoples of the sub-continent has been distorted by alien domination. They have still to find their bearings as independent nations. They still need to acquire confidence to break with the past.

To the end of his life, Mr. Nehru maintained that the resolution of the Jammu and Kashmir dispute would not bring peace and amity to the sub-continent, because Indo-Pakistani disputes were only the symptoms of the bigoted attitude of theocratic and reactionary Pakistan to secular, progressive India. Pakistan, on the other hand, maintained that only by a resolution of the disputes, to which the Indian Government and Prime Minister Nehru were internationally committed, would it be possible to determine whether the disputes were the causes or the symptoms of Indo-Pakistani differences. It is obvious that only by the resolution of territorial and other essential disputes could it be possible to attain normal conditions. It is strange logic to usurp the territorial and economic rights of a country on the grounds that enmity with that country is unavoidable. There is no

such thing as eternal enmity. Once disputes are equitably resolved, tensions give way to normal conditions. The chief
dispute between Pakistan and India hinges on the future of the
state of Jammu and Kashmir, to whose people India is in
honour bound to give the right of self-determination. It would
be wrong, however, to think that Kashmir is the only dispute
that divides India and Pakistan, though it is undoubtedly the
most significant. There have been others of considerable gravity,
such as the dispute over the canal waters, that over the future
of the Ganges waters, and that occasioned by the persecution of
Muslims in India, resulting in their emigration to Pakistan in
large numbers. Other problems again, for historical and other
reasons, have not been properly taken up, but remain nevertheless of fundamental national interest. One at least is nearly
as important as the Kashmir dispute: that of Assam and some
districts of India adjacent to East Pakistan. To these East
Pakistan has very good claims, which should not have been
allowed to remain quiescent. India has never ceased to take an
unpleasant interest in East Pakistan and continues to support
certain irredentist movements in West Pakistan. At a time when
the Nagas and the Mizos have revolted and thousands of
Muslims been ejected from Assam, which did not have a
majority Hindu community at the time of Partition, it would
be wrong of Pakistan to ignore these problems. The eviction of
Indian Muslims into East Pakistan and the disputed borders
of Assam and Tripura should not be forgotten. The future
of Farrakah barrage and the general problem of the uses of
rivers have yet to be equitably settled; and, although the
Nehru–Noon agreement was concluded ten years back, Beru-
bari has still to be transferred to Pakistan. Both wings of the
country have legitimate grievances against India and until the
principal disputes are resolved, it would be futile to expect
relations to improve.

Nehru's thesis that these disputes are a symptom of Pakistan's
eternal hostility towards India is as sinister as it is baseless, for
it is India and not Pakistan that harbours ill-will. Pakistan
achieved equality with India in the struggle for independence.
The Indian Congress Party resisted the partition of the country,
but failed to prevent the establishment of Pakistan. It is thus
natural that some Indian leaders should continue to nurture

grievances against Pakistan. Only because India persists in not permitting the completion of Pakistan have relations between the two countries deteriorated into their present hopeless deadlock. The philosophy of Pakistan is based on the equality of man and on the concept of Islamic justice; and it would be a negation of this philosophy for Pakistan to harbour animosity towards her principal neighbour.

Muslims ruled the sub-continent for over 700 years and eventually succeeded in establishing their separate homeland. Unfortunately, the Indian mentality is troubled with historical complexes and the obsession of defeat. In order to go to the roots of Indo-Pakistani relations, one must examine the nature of Indian nationalism.

From the time of the *Rig Vedas*, the dominant features of the Indian genius have been its religious temperament and an exclusiveness derived from the caste system. Although Indian civilization is considered synonymous with Hindu culture, it has shown, over the centuries, a remarkable capacity for assimilating alien cultures. An impressive pre-Aryan civilization lies buried in the Indus Valley among the ruins of Mohenjo Daro and Harappa. It is often forgotten that it was on the ruins of this civilization that the Aryan invaders established their new order, which led to the birth of Hindu-Brahmanism. As the Aryan invaders spread from the plains of the north-west to the upper regions of the Ganges, the historical centre of gravity shifted from the Indus Valley and the Panjab to the Gangetic Valley, and the Vedic age gave place to the era of Brahmanism.

The *Rig Vedas* record the existence of the two races: the high-spirited Dravidians, who were engaged in a life-and-death struggle to defend their homeland; and the invading Aryans, the fair-skinned aliens. The Aryan rulers arrogated to themselves the attributes of *Dewas* or gods, and the indigenous people were classified as *Rakhasas* or devils. The caste system was a product of the Brahmanic concept of superiority, which came to be accepted as a way of life. Even the *Shudras*, or low-caste Hindus, were accorded some distinction from the *Malech* or non-Aryan; although both categories were excluded from domestic, civil, and military honours in this life and denied *Mukti* or salvation in the life hereafter. With the advent of the Scythian invaders, Brahmanism suffered a setback. The Scythian rulers were content with the nominal subjugation of the local population. They did not establish their own code of exclusive prerogatives in the domain of religion. The Brahmans continued to flourish, bowing before their new masters, but stoutly refusing to admit them within their social or religious domains. At this time was born the great Buddha, a Scythian prince. 'All men are equal, and salvation is equally open to all', declared Lord Buddha, to the horror of the Brahmans. Buddhism had to pay later the price of banishment from India. Jainism, which followed in the wake of the decline of Buddhistic influence, nearly met the same fate at the hands of the Brahmans.

A cursory examination of Indian history reveals how Hinduism has handled the incursions of external elements. Minor inroads have been repaired by assimilation; conquerors have been seduced by subservience; and those among the conquerors who have remained in India have escaped assimilation only by assiduous efforts to retain their separate identity.

This proud Indian order was broken by the Muslim conquest. The blow had to be endured, but defiance was offered consistently in the name of *Dharma*. The Indian order was not slow to perceive that, unlike other invading tribes, the Muslims were no barbarians to be readily assimilated. They did not consider admission to the indigenous polity a promotion, and so began the tragic Hindu–Muslim confrontation. Throughout the period of Muslim domination, the Hindu exhibited an intense pride of race and culture, which developed into violent xenophobia. All the hatred and fear associated with the notion of *Malech*— the unclean and uncivilized foreigner—were invoked in the struggle against the Muslim alien. Even when the Muslims sought compromise by adopting Indian ways and by marrying Indian women, they could not be accepted as equals because the faith of Islam was a challenge to the fundamental concept of the Hindu dogma. This militant spirit was freely invoked in countless uprisings against the Muslims.

One of the earlier attempts on the part of a conqueror to come to terms with Hinduism was made by Akbar, but his objectives were neutralized by the sheer weight of Hindu dogma, which prevented a *modus vivendi* between the two communities. His policy of co-operation, however, gave the Hindus the opportunity to influence and encircle the Muslim élite. Aurangzeb thought it necessary to react by reversing the process, but came too late to complete his mission. By the time he ascended the throne, the Mughal Empire was in the throes of decay. He had to save the Empire, fight the Marathas, and face many other harassing problems.

It was to fight the colonial domination of the British that a more consistent policy of assimilation was instituted by leaders of the National Congress. In both the 1857 War of Independence and the Khilafat Movement Hindus and Muslims fought side by side against British domination to achieve their common objectives. In each case, however, when the struggle reached a critical stage, their unity could not be sustained, with the result that the movements were suppressed. Neither the Mughal attempt to work out a relationship of equality nor the common cause against imperialism was able to sustain co-operation leading to a lasting unity.

Eminent historians, who have exercised a powerful influence over the Indian mind, have elaborated the concept of Mother India as not only the Motherland, but also the Holy Land of the Hindus from the Himalayas to Cape Comorin. This veneration for *Bharat-Mata*, which is *Arya-Varta* (Aryan homeland), is the central theme of Hinduism, the strangest welter of mythology, philosophy, cosmogony, and religion that the world has ever seen. The Aryans, from whom the Brahmans claim their descent, lived for many centuries in the Panjab before they advanced eastwards across northern India, conquering the indigenous Dasyus. The earliest Hindu holy scriptures, the *Rig Vedas* and the *Upanishads*, were composed by the *Rishis*, or ancient sages, in the Panjab.

In the Hindu national consciousness, as inspired by many great Hindu writers of the last century, the sub-continent is conceived as a unity—one and indivisible from the Khyber Hills to the far south, with the North-West, which is now Pakistan, its heart and soul. Geographical India was never completely united under one rule, except that of the British and nominally for a few years under the Mughal Emperor Aurangzeb. Before that, the first Indian Empire, that of the Mauryas, had extended over the whole of northern India, reaching into Afghanistan and some parts of the southern peninsula. Indian influence spread eastwards across the ocean to Cambodia and

Java. Brahmanical religious and cultural influence was more extensive than the frontiers of any single Indian Empire in the past. The Hindu religion expressly extols the concept of *Chaptrapati* or the Lord Paramount, a ruler who conquers and dominates his neighbours and extends his sway from ocean to ocean. This kind of consciousness of past greatness, regenerated by Indian writers to inspire Hindu cultural and political revival, has been the mainspring of twentieth-century Indian nationalism. Nehru's *Discovery of India* shows how the most westernized of Hindu minds fell captive to this spell of the 'essential Hinduness of India'.

The advent of Islam in force in the eleventh century brought not only a loss of political power, but also outrage to the dominant religion. An Indian author, analysing the reasons for the Hindu–Muslim conflict, observes:

The Muslim conquest of India could not be made innocuous for the Hindus through the caste system. The conquest was an extension into a new country of a well-established and mature society, with a fully developed way of life and a living culture. The final conquest of India was the adventure of a Muslim King whose main territories lay outside India, but even when the subordination of the new Muslim empire to an external Muslim Kingdom was ended, as it very soon was, Muslim rule in the country remained the rule of a colonizing people who never forgot their affiliation with the wider Islamic world.

What was even more important was the fact that the Muslims were not barbarians at a low level of culture who would consider admission to the Hindu fold as a promotion. On the contrary, not only were they themselves the creators and defenders of a new and aggressive culture, they had a fanatical conviction of its superiority to all others, and thought it was their duty to propagate it even by force. Their religion did, in fact, make this one of the essential, though optional, duties of a Muslim. They were the first people in history to put forward the idea of an irreconcilable conflict between a particular way of life and all others, and to formulate a theory of permanent revolution. There could be no peace on earth, they declared, until the whole world was converted to their faith.

As if that was not enough, the Hindus on their side had an almost equal contribution to make. By the time the new invasions began, they had, as I have noted, completely lost whatever assimilating power and adaptability they had and hardened into a closed

M

society with a conviction of its own superiority which amounted to megalomania. There could thus be no question of absorbing even a neutral foreigner, let alone a Muslim.[1]

Fed on centuries of hatred, their sense of injury received at Muslim hands reinforced by religious dogma, all Hindu movements have conceived the assimilation of the Muslim minority as part of their political objective; differing only as to their methods. The Hindu Mahasabha and the RSSS (Rastriya Swaya Sevak Sangh) were committed to violence and the forcible conversion of Muslims into the lowest strata of Indian society. Gandhi's methods were more subtle. He frequently spoke of Muslims as blood-brothers and held out innumerable assurances that their rights would be safeguarded under a Congress-governed India; but whenever called upon to define their rights and share of political power in an independent India, he invariably evaded a clear answer. Nehru, with his background of association with Muslim culture, not to speak of his Cambridge education and avowal of Marxist philosophy, dismissed the fact of a separate Muslim culture in the subcontinent. He asked, 'What is this Muslim culture? Is it Persian–Aryan culture or the Arab Semitic one?' The only difference between a Hindu and a Muslim that he could discern was that the Hindu wore the dhoti and the Muslim a pyjama and a Turkish fez.

Nirad C. Chaudhuri writes of Hindu militancy:

Life-long observation has convinced me that there is a streak of insanity in the Hindus and that nobody will arrive at a correct appraisement of Hindu private and public behaviour on the supposition that they have a normal personality. This madness lurks within their ordinary workaday self like a monomania, and the nature of the alienation can even be defined in the psychiatrist's terms—it is partly dementia praecox, and partly paranoia. In all Hindu activities, especially in the public sphere, can be detected clear signs of either a feebleness of mental faculties or a perversion of them.

If anyone scouts this hypothesis I would ask him to remember the recent history of the German and the Japanese people when they forced disastrous wars on mankind. No other supposition except temporary collective insanity can account for the Nazi phase of

[1] Nirad C. Chaudhuri, *The Continent of Circe*, 1965, p. 63.

German history or the courting of a war with the United States by the Japanese. These examples led me to the conclusion that human groups, like individuals, can go mad. I have only extended the view to the Hindus. But the Hindus show two important differences in their collective madness: first, their insane behaviour is feebler in expression and therefore less catastrophic for the rest of mankind, though very harmful to themselves; secondly, it is continuous and permanent, and cannot be expected to pass off as the German and the Japanese madness has done.[1]

The Muslim League was founded in 1906, significantly, during a period of extremist ascendency in the Congress. A key-Congress word during the 1920s and 1930s was *Sangatan*, solidarity, integration, consolidation. The RSSS was founded in Magpur in 1925. In 1923, when the late Maulana Mohammad Ali was collaborating with Gandhi in the famous Khilafat Movement, V. D. Savarkar published *Hindustava*, a book which has influenced Hindu nationalists up to the present day. Savarkar's definition of 'Hindu' is revealing: 'A Hindu means a person who regards this land of Bharatvarsha, from the Indus to the Seas as his Fatherland as well as his Holy land, that is, the cradle or land of his religion. "Hindustava" embraces all the departments of thought and activity of the whole being of our Hindu race.'[2] The Hindus were a nation; the Muslims only a community.

Now that the Muslim has succeeded in carving out a home for himself, he poses a greater challenge to Hinduism. Pakistan is considered a cruel mutilation of *Bharat-Mata*, and Hindu militarism is straining at the leash. Patel once declared that if India so desired she could sweep up to Peshawar. Between 1947 and 1954 she was prevented twice, if not three times, from undertaking such an adventure for fear of international censure and repercussions. In 1965, however, came the treacherous attack; Indian militarism being under the chauvinistic illusion that it would be able to overwhelm Pakistan.

The Indian leaders agreed to Pakistan only when it became clear to them that partition was inevitable and that they had to concede to this division as a price for the transference of power from British to Indian hands. Even while agreeing to Pakistan,

---

[1] ibid., pp. 117–18.
[2] *Hindustava*, 1942, p. 4.

Gandhi, Nehru, Patel, and the others never really conceded the two-nation theory. They accepted partition as a matter of bitter expediency, in the hope and expectation that the new State would not be viable and would collapse under pressure from its larger and more powerful neighbour.

India's attitude towards Pakistan since Independence is well known. The seizure of Junagadh, Kashmir, and Hyderabad is too fresh in our memory to need recapitulation. It has never seemed to India a contradiction that, while she laid claim to Junagadh and Hyderabad by reason of the overwhelming Hindu composition of the population, she rejected the same criterion in the case of Jammu and Kashmir with their over-whelming Muslim population. Instead, Indian leaders intro-duced the falsely applied concepts of secularism and democracy and the hostage theory to deny to the people of Jammu and Kashmir their inalienable rights.

In the light of these historical and psychological factors which govern the Indian attitude towards Pakistan, it is clear that Indian leaders have come to tolerate Pakistan, because they do not have the power to destroy her. If they could forge this power, as they are endeavouring to do by the augmentation of their military forces, they would end partition and reabsorb Pakistan into the India of their dreams. They have pronounced Pakistan their chief enemy. The whole aim of Indian diplomacy under Nehru and his successors has been to isolate our country so that, when India has built up sufficient strength, she could overwhelm and absorb us as quickly and quietly as possible.

The founder of Pakistan, Mohammad Ali Jinnah, was known as 'The Ambassador of Hindu–Muslim Unity' and the Indian National Congress regarded him as an apostle of their move-ment. At the height of his career he did his utmost, with all the fervour and enthusiasm of his earlier days, to promote the cause of Indian independence, so that Hindu and Muslim could live side by side within a single polity and find their emancipation under one roof. The fact that he failed is in itself significant. Failure as such would have depressed a lesser man. Mr. Jinnah, whose singlemindedness and stamina have become a legend, could hardly have been deterred by failure alone. Experience had shown him that the Indian leaders sought the co-operation of Muslims not as equals, but only as a means to eliminate their identity. For some years he remained abroad, aloof from the tortuous course of Indian politics. Only when approached by such Muslim leaders as Maulana Mohammad Ali did he return to fulfil his historic mission. Enriched by his earlier experience, he then adopted the only logical course open to him: exposure of the Congress ambitions to subjugate the Muslims of the sub-continent. For the Muslim League he formulated a policy of total confrontation, steadfastly refusing to succumb to the lures and promises of co-operation with which Congress sought to distract or entice him. He was relentless in the pursuit of his objectives and would not be deflected from his course by either the sweet words of Sarojini Naidu or the hypnotic dialectics of Gandhi.

In abandoning his advocacy of Hindu–Muslim unity, the founder of Pakistan left us a lesson which has, with the passage of time, become clearer in its relevance. The fact that the Hindus and Muslims of the sub-continent constituted two separate nationalities formed the foundation of the edifice of Pakistan. When this was first propounded as the Muslims' political objective, the leaders of the Muslim League were ridiculed not only by the Indian National Congress and the British, but also by many eminent Muslims. It seemed to them preposterous that, after nearly two hundred years of united existence under one yoke as the most precious gem in the Crown of the British Empire, the country should be rent asunder. Subsequent events are now a part of history. Pakistan was achieved as a result of an overwhelming popular decision, in which the Muslims of the sub-continent, including those who knew that they would not form a part of Pakistan, cast their votes for its creation.

At this stage, it might be useful to examine the considerations which influenced the abdicating power. Britain had decided that it was no longer feasible to continue her colonial rule, but was not unaware of the need to protect her own considerable interests after the liquidation of the Empire. The partition of British India had to be consistent with British residual interests, successor states being established in a manner favourable to Britain's post-imperial objectives. Through India's devoted spokesman, Lord Mountbatten, Britain succeeded not only in bringing about a truncation of Pakistan, but also in furnishing India with massive advantages against Pakistan. Referenda

were held in the North-West Frontier Province and in the district
of Sylhet in East Pakistan. The results in both cases were over-
whelmingly in favour of Pakistan. Kalat was advised to declare
its independence along with the adjacent territories of Baluchistan. The British Government, however, took every possible
opportunity to increase the imbalance against Pakistan. The
Punjab was partitioned and, in violation of the principle of
partition according to the composition of population in contiguous regions, vast Muslim-populated territories stretching up to
the fringes of Amritsar and including Gurdaspur and Ferozepur
were arbitrarily handed over to India. Assam was relinquished,
Bengal partitioned, and India was granted corridors allowing
access to Jammu and Kashmir in the north and to Assam and
Tripura in the east. In North Bengal, such a corridor leading to
Assam provided India with an uninterrupted contiguity with
the southern boundaries of Nepal and gave her access to the
Himalayan states of Sikkim and Bhutan bordering on China.
In no instance was the benefit of doubt given to Pakistan in the
division of territory or its other claims.

In the circumstances prevailing in the sub-continent at that
time, the British Government could not have done more to
tilt the balance of advantage in India's favour. The transfer of
power was peacefully determined as a result of agreement between the British Government, the Indian National Congress,
and the Muslim League; but the manner in which the transfer
was effected by the ruling power betrayed prejudice against
Pakistan. No attempt was made to provide Pakistan with the
minimum requirements for administration, defence, and finance.
The country was left to fend for herself. In the maintenance of
law and order, the division of assets, military stores, and sterling
balances, and even in the transfer of funds, India was given a
stranglehold over Pakistan. It was intended to punish the
Muslims for winning self-determination by giving them a weak
and emasculated state which would quickly wither away in the
non-Marxian sense.

It is not difficult to see why India has been strengthened in
the belief that an isolated Pakistan would be to her advantage.
When almost the entire Muslim population of the sub-continent
voted for Pakistan, it voted in fact for a Pakistan consisting of
the Provinces of Panjab, Sind, Baluchistan, and the North-West

Frontier Province in the west, and for Bengal and Assam in the east, together with the Princely States having Muslim majorities. India felt she could liquidate, in the course of time, the truncated Pakistan that finally emerged. East Pakistan was considered particularly vulnerable and so forces of disruption and subversion were let loose there, but India had not bargained on the determination, patriotism, and pride of our nation. Indian economists made a cynical assessment of the economic viability of Pakistan. They believed the country could not survive the rupture of its trade and economic relations with India. On the basis of this assessment India forced an economic blockade on Pakistan, but Pakistan reacted bravely. Foreign trade was boosted, the processing of indigenous raw material was undertaken and, having withstood the initial dislocation, Pakistan was able to move on to a new era in which her economy became progressively more capable of withstanding India's economic aggression. In surmounting these problems, it was the single-mindedness of her people that saved the country. If Pakistan had weakened in her resolve, India would have tightened her grip in many other ways. Fortunately, Pakistan did not weaken, and not only broke the economic blockade, but took positive steps to make its economy more independent of India.

Every conceivable situation in our internal affairs continues to be exploited by India with the aim of aggravating our difficulties and weakening our national integrity. It is no coincidence that the genesis of every Indo-Pakistani dispute lies in a definite act of Indian hostility. The origin of the Jammu and Kashmir dispute, the events leading to the United Nations resolutions of 1948 and 1949, the numerous mediation attempts by the United Nations and others, bilateral negotiations, India's repeated attempts to frustrate any settlement and, finally, her renunciation of solemn international commitments, tell a tale of consistent ill-will.

Her policy of evictions leaves no doubt that India's principal objective is the obliteration of Pakistan. The meanest intellect in the sub-continent must now be aware of the vicious circle of communal disturbance, exodus, repercussion, and exodus in the reverse direction. It is axiomatic in our circumstances that oppression of minorities in one country has inevitable ramifications in the other. Moreover, it is highly probable that, if as a result of such oppression, any significant migration ensues, it would provoke the majority community, cause unrest among members of the minority community and create a law and order crisis of grave magnitude. India formulated a deliberate and well-planned policy of harassing and evicting the Muslims of Assam. Thousands were torn from their homes and pushed across the border with a complete disregard not only for their fundamental human rights, but also for the resultant turmoil. The long series of communal riots in India have kept more than sixty million Muslims in the country in a state of perpetual fear. In the winter of 1963–4, the outbreak of rioting, looting, and arson cost many Muslim lives in West Bengal alone and set in motion a fresh wave of exodus of Muslims into East Pakistan. Notwithstanding every possible precaution of the Government of Pakistan, there were lamentable episodes in which enraged Muslims wreaked their vengeance on members of the minority community.

The fact that India carried out a deliberate policy of evicting its Muslim minority, causing untold misery both to the direct victims and to the Hindu minority in Pakistan, is a matter of special significance. The objective is not difficult to understand. East Pakistan, which India failed to subvert, was to be kept under constant pressure from the outside. By evicting Indian Muslims they would not only subject East Pakistan to the physical pressure of having to rehabilitate thousands, but it would also confront Pakistan with the responsibilities of ensuring the protection of its Hindu minority. This dual pressure was designed to weaken East Pakistan and keep things perpetually on the boil. More than five million Muslims from India have been forced into East Pakistan in this process, which has strained our economy considerably and caused new tensions and problems of law and order. The war which was launched across the international frontier against Lahore on 6 September 1965 is a landmark in the history of Indo-Pakistani relations. On this date India finally passed the point of no return.

From time immemorial the exponents of Greater Bharat have maintained that its political, cultural, and economic hegemony should extend from the Hindukush to the Mekong. Throughout Indian history political philosophers have propounded this theme at such length and with such frequency that it has become a part of the tradition which modern India has inherited. The fact that it is nearly a thousand years since India was in a position to take any step towards that glorious objective has not diminished either the intensity or the extent of this unwavering ambition. As a first step towards its realization, Pakistan must be neutralized, but ultimately the semi-religious concept of *Akhand Bharat* demands the end of Pakistan itself.

CHAPTER 19

Confrontation with India

The principal objective of Indian foreign policy has been to isolate Pakistan. In the early days, recognizing the fact that Pakistan had affinities with the Middle East, India concentrated her diplomatic activity against Pakistan in the Arab World. When, in self-defence, we moved towards the United States, India denounced our mutual Defence Agreements with that country.

Taking advantage of Soviet hostility toward CENTO, India embarked on a comprehensive plan for co-operation with the Soviet Union in political, economic, and military matters, firstly, to counteract Pakistan's alliance with Western countries, and, secondly, to put further difficulties in the way of Soviet–Pakistan relations. India's initial objective was the promotion of grandiose designs in south-east Asia and the total isolation of Pakistan from the People's Republic of China. In international organizations, such as the United Nations, India continued to operate on an over-ambitious scale and, for the benefit of the Afro-Asian world, sought to portray Pakistan as a client of the Western Powers and, therefore, unsuited to play an important role in Afro-Asian matters. Perhaps the excess of zeal with which India pursued this objective helped Pakistan to maintain her standing in the international arena. It became increasingly clear to other countries that it was India's malice towards Pakistan and not the substance of Pakistan's domestic or foreign policy which motivated Indian policy. Her obduracy over the Jammu and Kashmir dispute did more than any other factor to expose the true nature of her policies towards Pakistan. This unconcern for international morality led India to a position in which, during the war between India and Pakistan, her leaders were forced to lament their isolation and the lack of support from any part of the world.

On the one hand, India preached peace, while on the other, she continued to increase her defence expenditure to unprecedented levels. On the one hand, she preached non-alignment as the moral basis for her external policies, while on the other, she continued to exploit both power blocs for her own purposes. She professed herself a friend of the underdeveloped world, but at the same time continued to clothe herself in the mantle of the receding colonial Powers. Such contradictions exposed her in her true colours. All evidence points to the fact that it is India, not Pakistan, that cannot arrive at a fair reconciliation. Whereas Pakistan maintains the confrontation only to resolve the outstanding disputes, India seeks the absorption of Pakistan for the return of normal conditions.

It has been suggested that Pakistan should become realistic and seek *rapprochement* with India without the settlement of outstanding disputes. Even this would not resolve the dilemma. Pakistan has already lost valuable territories to India under pretext of realism and, if applied to Jammu and Kashmir and other disputes, this process would involve the territorial attrition of our country. It would mean capitulation by instalment and eventual liquidation. By settlement of a dispute we mean a solution designed to achieve lasting peace. Only through an equitable settlement can such an honourable peace be secured and, if it is our fundamental objective to achieve this, as it should be, then we must consider how it is to be achieved. Can it be achieved on India's terms? Certainly not; because if India's terms were to prevail, there would be no viable Pakistan. If the worst were to come to the worst, what would be the consequences of Pakistan abandoning Jammu and Kashmir? It is clear that a compromise of this nature would whet but not satisfy India's appetite and, with her growing military power and possible acquisition of nuclear weapons, she would use these territories as a rallying point to integrate the remaining parts of Pakistan.

At the time of partition, Pakistan lost Gurdaspur, Ferozepur, and certain other parts of the Panjab as well as valuable territories in the eastern part, notably in Assam and Tripura. Likewise, in Amritsar district, Muslim majority areas spread from Lahore district to the suburbs of the city of Amritsar. All these extensive and valuable territories were arbitrarily and unjustly given to India to further strengthen that country at the cost of Pakistan. These areas were the granary of the north and were very important strategically. By giving them to India, the defence of Lahore and other parts of West Pakistan became badly exposed. At that time, it was argued that such were the anomalies of the upheavals of partition and revolution, that it was better to accept and consolidate a truncated Pakistan than fight for territories lost through an iniquitous foreign award. India's occupation of Junagadh and Hyderabad created political and psychological conditions which were of incalculable advantage to her. She was confirmed in her belief that, by the threat and use of force as a deliberate instrument of her foreign policy, she could make Pakistan submit to all her policies. The Jammu and Kashmir dispute has continued for over twenty years, and the question is now whether Pakistan has the courage and endurance to continue to uphold the right of this subjugated people, or whether its stamina is weakening under heavy external pressure. When we are told that India is too large to be resisted, that fifty-five million people in East Pakistan should not sacrifice themselves for the five million people in Kashmir, or that the people of West Pakistan should not resist the Indian occupation of Kashmir, thereby exposing their limited territorial depth to a military onslaught, it indicates erosion of the national resolve.

The argument of comparative numbers can be reduced to a logical absurdity. Let us say that the population of Pakistan is one hundred million. When would a nation of this size be prepared to risk liberating territory and a related population from the enemy? Would it be prepared to take the risk only when the population to be liberated becomes one hundred and one million? But then it would not be a war of liberation, but rather a war of conquest, in other words a colonial war. The argument that numerical disparity justifies inaction is patently false and ignores the many other causes of discord between India and Pakistan. Our countries must ultimately live in peace, but only when the conflict has been resolved. Such peaceful co-existence, however, remains out of the question so long as India strives to impose a cultural, religious, and linguistic uniformity upon all its minorities. The surrender of Pakistan's interest does not resolve the conflict. If we are not prepared to expose our people and territory to risk, then we must expect our frontiers with India to be eroded, each erosion by itself being too small to provoke a suitable response. In international politics, as in science, the so-called commonsense argument is not always valid. Science began to progress when *a priori* arguments from commonsense ceased to be honoured; as, for example, when Galileo proved, against all the rules of commonsense, that light and heavy bodies fall to earth at the same speed. In international politics, so many factors are involved that an ideal solution is rarely found, since variables of the kind that involve human beings are subject to human decisions. When France was overrun in the Second World War, had the British been devotees of commonsense arguments, they would have yielded to the Germans; but Churchill did not do so. He offered his country blood, toil, tears, and sweat, and Britain won the war.

On the basis of the argument that a struggle for a part of the nation's territory is not worth the sacrifice of the whole nation, India might be permitted to take over Karachi and Sind as a result of some territorial usurpation. Would it be prudent for the rest of the population of Pakistan to sacrifice what remains of their country for the ten million people of Karachi and Sind? Next might come the turn of Baluchistan; then that of the remaining parts of East and West Pakistan, to complete the country's piecemeal liquidation. If this premise is to be applied to Jammu and Kashmir which, to the people of Pakistan, is as much a part of their country as is Rawalpindi or Chittagong, it can be applied to all other territories as well. The issue is not a complicated one, nor should we allow it to become so. India is the larger country, but it is beset with terrifying problems; we, though smaller, have in our hands the potent weapon of a just cause. On balance, our advantages and disadvantages are equally divided or, if anything, incline in Pakistan's favour. The sub-continent is not likely to face another blood-bath. Internal and external conditions cannot permit it, but this does not mean that we should not be prepared to make sacrifices. Even without the solution of the Jammu and Kashmir problem, blood is being spilled there every day. There are cease-fire violations. Muslims are being tortured and evicted in the eastern region of India. People are suffering and dying needlessly despite the Tashkent Agreement and the United Nations.

Why does India want Jammu and Kashmir? She holds them because their valley is the handsome head of the body of

Pakistan. Its possession enables her to cripple the economy of West Pakistan and, militarily, to dominate the country. India retains Jammu and Kashmir because she wants to increase her strategic importance by having common borders with the Soviet Union and China, and correspondingly denying Pakistan these frontiers. Above all, she retains the state against all norms of morality because she wants to negate the two-nation theory, the basis of Pakistan. If a Muslim majority area can remain a part of India, then the *raison d'être* of Pakistan collapses. These are the reasons why India, to continue her domination of Jammu and Kashmir, defies international opinion and violates her pledges. For the same reasons, Pakistan must continue unremittingly her struggle for the right of self-determination of this subject people. Pakistan is incomplete without Jammu and Kashmir both territorially and ideologically. Recovering them, she would recover her head and be made whole, stronger, and more viable. It would be fatal if, in sheer exhaustion or out of intimidation, Pakistan were to abandon the struggle, and a bad compromise would be tantamount to abandonment; which might, in turn, lead to the collapse of Pakistan. If, however, we settle for tranquil relations with India, without an equitable resolution of disputes, it would be the first major step in establishing Indian leadership in our parts, with Pakistan and other neighbouring states becoming Indian satellites.

It has taken twenty years and two wars to establish the separate identity of our state with its population of over a hundred and twenty million, yet there are people who still lament the partition of the sub-continent, portraying Pakistan as the prodigal son who will some day return to the bosom of *Bharat-Mata*. Either under external influence or in the light of her experience, India has, after the September war of 1965, begun to talk of co-operation with Pakistan. What does she seek to gain from this change in tactics? To improve her economic position by reducing her heavy defence expenditure; to gain a breathing space in which to deal firmly with dissident elements. She would like to crush the Nagas and Mizos, who are close to East Pakistan, suppress the south and the Sikhs, contain pockets of discontent in Rajputana, and break the spirit of sixty million Indian Muslims.

It has often been said that the future of Indian Muslims would be endangered if relations between Pakistan and India remain in a state of confrontation. This argument is used to blackmail Pakistan and to hold the Indian Muslims in perpetual fear as hostages in India's policy of aggression and aggrandizement. A deeper study of the problem reveals that the reverse is closer to the truth. A strong and determined Pakistan, refusing to surrender one millimetre of her legitimate rights, is their best protection. The Muslims of the sub-continent voluntarily voted for Pakistan. The massive vote in favour of partition was cast as much by those who were to remain in India as by those in territories which were to form Pakistan. The confidence of the Muslims reached a climax when Mr. Jinnah confronted the Indian leaders with the two-nation theory. India turned on her own Muslim citizens only after Partition; only when she believed that a weak and unstable Pakistan was in no position to retaliate. There can be no doubt that a weakened Pakistan would embolden India to discriminate further against Indian Muslims. Conversely, a strong Pakistan is their strongest guarantee of protection, since India would hesitate so to provoke an alert, vigorous Pakistan. It is not at all fortuitous that now, for the first time since her independence twenty years ago, at the height of the confrontation, and as a consequence of the war, India has elected a Muslim as her President. If, however, the sovereign State of Pakistan were to weaken, the Indian Government would feel freer to deal as it pleased with its minority groups. In such a situation the Indian Muslims would suffer gravely, but the immediate and worst-treated victims would be the Muslims of Jammu and Kashmir. The moment co-operation begins with India, without an equitable settlement of disputes, the people of Kashmir will naturally conclude that Pakistan has abandoned them, leaving them no option but to surrender to Indian aggression. If Pakistan, as a sovereign and well-armed state, destroys her power of resistance, how can the unarmed people of Jammu and Kashmir be expected to resist? After Pakistan's submission, India would feel free to bring the Himalayan states of Sikkim and Bhutan to heel and would coerce Nepal and Ceylon as well. With her hegemony spread from end to end of the sub-continent, India would then attempt to destroy for all time the possibility of another movement for Muslim self-determination.

With Pakistan co-operating on terms of inequality and submission, India would, in the first instance, turn her attention to
the rich and alluvial portion of East Pakistan, which would be
assailed with propaganda and subjected to economic and cultural encroachments. India would attempt, by threats and
seduction, by insidious cultural infiltration, by sheer weight of
proximity, to absorb East Pakistan into West Bengal. The
present theme of Indian propaganda is that the fifty-five million
people of East Pakistan should not sacrifice their future and be
exploited for the sake of the five million of Jammu and Kashmir,
who are, it is said, as close to East Pakistan as are, say, the
Muslims of Iran and Iraq. Were India to succeed in absorbing
Kashmir, she would advise East Pakistanis to regard the people
of West Pakistan as concerning them as little as the people of
Kashmir. Incessant appeals would be made to East Pakistan
to end the 'domination' of West Pakistan. Influential people
would be found in West Pakistan to argue in favour of East
Pakistan's separation. Such *agents provocateurs*, who are to be
found in any country, would propagate the idea that East
Pakistan is a 'liability' and that its 'blackmail' should be put
to an end by a final parting of the ways. Once the national
resolve to liberate Jammu and Kashmir is broken, subversion
to break the link between them would increase in both wings.
If, in this way, Pakistan were to be divided, each wing would
immediately lose its importance by half. Instead of being two
mighty pillars of strength in the sub-continent, Pakistan would
be reduced to two weak states. The process of disintegration
would continue until East Pakistan were absorbed into West
Bengal and would provide an encouraging example to sep-
aratist movements in West Pakistan.

India tried to prevent Pakistan's coming into being, but
failed. After Independence, she imposed an economic blockade
in order to destroy our economy, a manœuvre that not only
failed to break, but actually strengthened Pakistan. The September war of 1965 has now convinced India that she cannot
destroy Pakistan by confrontation. Her policy will therefore
shift from confrontation to co-operation, to the 'Spirit of Tashkent'. She will now seek to convert Pakistan into her satellite by
holding out inducements of peaceful co-operation. It is a more
subtle approach. How can any sensible person object to it? It

would appear unreasonable to ignore the extended hand of friendship. India, however, plans to enter by the back door, like a burglar. In this she would be aided and abetted by foreign Powers. The point of departure between India's objective to absorb Pakistan and the United States' objective is reached the moment the latter presses for aggressive confrontation with China. India's own efforts would be directed to obtaining the submission of Pakistan for her own greater glory and not as prelude to a provocative encirclement of China. India's objective and that of the United States in seeking Pakistan's submission have one interest in common, but are in conflict in respect of another. If Pakistan assesses the situation correctly, she can bring them to cancel one another; if, on the other hand, Pakistan yields to pressure, the result would be greater co-operation between India and the United States, which would remove the contradictions, to the extent at least of hastening Pakistan's submission to India.

Thus, India would welcome the proposals for joint ventures, yet hesitate to adopt them. She would welcome the proposals for the purpose of absorbing Pakistan, but would be inhibited if the object is to bring about the co-operation in order to confront China. History holds no precedent of successful joint economic ventures between states with unresolved territorial and other fundamental disputes. It would be like asking UAR or Syria to embark on joint ventures with Israel in their region. Some foreign experts have, on the other hand, said there are two economies in Pakistan and, on the other, emphasis is placed on the complementary nature of the economies of East Pakistan and West Bengal. In other words, internally, as a nation, Pakistan has two economies, but externally the eastern part of Pakistan has an indivisible economy with a part of India! Without the settlement of disputes, and in disregard of the principles relevant to the protection of sovereign rights, the World Bank wants to intervene high-handedly to impose a solution for the utilization of the waters of the Ganges. It wants to bring about co-operation between the two countries by making East Pakistan share its waters with West Bengal and vice versa. The analogy of the Indus Basin Treaty does not hold. This was intended to divide the waters between India and Pakistan to decrease interdependence. In the case of East Pakistan, efforts are being made to impose a solution which would make East Pakistan dependent on West Bengal. Such a solution would place Pakistan at the mercy of West Bengal with inevitable and disastrous consequences. With this precedent, other projects would follow for joint participation in hydro-electric schemes leading to collaboration in agriculture and industry. The proposal for the reduction of armed forces has already been dealt with, but, even in this case, apart from all other drawbacks which have been discussed, India could always circumvent such an agreement by exaggerating the threat of China, in connivance with the United States. If that becomes difficult, efforts would be made to supply India with arms from other satellite countries to make the agreement inapplicable to India.

CHAPTER 20

Epilogue

No country in the world can in principle oppose universal disarmament in face of the ever-present risk of the employment of thermo-nuclear weapons on a scale to destroy life on this planet. When people everywhere are anxious to improve their living conditions, no nation has the right to oppose the demand for using available resources for economic development instead of defence. However, in order to be effective, disarmament must be on a multilateral, universal basis, so that no one nation has an advantage over another, or one group of nations an advantage over another group of nations. But the proposal for the reduction of forces between India and Pakistan does not contain a single element of equity. India is in possession of Jammu and Kashmir and eastern enclaves belonging to Pakistan. In such circumstances, bilateral disarmament between India and Pakistan would mean the victory of the state possessing the disputed territory and the defeat of the dispossessed.

We should not be daunted by the powerful support India is getting. By herself she is a menace to the security of Pakistan and, aided by powerful external forces, she will be a greater menace. But no matter how great the menace, it cannot break the united resolve of a nation with a just cause. The present situation cannot last indefinitely. The attitudes of Global Powers, as we have seen, are capable of changing. In international dealings there is no such thing as an 'irrevocable constant'. That is why India is afraid when she hears talk about bridges of understanding between China and the United States. With the passage of time, when a *modus vivendi* is struck between the United States and China, or between China and the Soviet Union, India will find herself in isolation. The war in Vietnam is of decisive importance. It has a direct bearing on future developments in the sub-continent and in Asia as a whole. Let us hope that it does not extend, giving us the respite to resolve our problems satisfactorily. The growing United States–China confrontation over Vietnam appears, at first sight, to have an adverse effect on Pakistan, but a closer examination dispels this notion. We could find the situation in Vietnam of help in overcoming the mounting pressures if we are able to resist those that are already felt. If that war ends satisfactorily, it might lead to a reduction in the tensions between the United States and China, which would be to Pakistan's advantage. If the war continues, the United States is likely to become so completely involved as to be unable to exert further pressure on Pakistan; nor, in the prevailing conditions, will it want to precipitate another serious crisis in Asia.

In any event, whether the United States is or is not capable of imposing its conditions, there should be no doubt that Pakistan will hold its ground, reject all obnoxious conditions, and resolutely resist foreign interference. She should continue to confront India until there is a satisfactory settlement of territorial and other fundamental disputes bearing on East and West Pakistan.

It would be wrong, however, to conclude that under no circumstances would Pakistan want to co-operate with India. The bonds of geography, history, and culture are not to be denied. In view of our eagerness to improve our relations with remote countries and neighbours alike, it would be natural to try to improve relations with India. However, in order to be productive, co-operation must be on the basis of true equality between nations which have no prejudices against each other and no territorial or other fundamental disputes. Co-operation cannot co-exist with injustice. Would it have been possible for the British to co-operate on the basis of inequality and domination with the India people before Independence or for France to co-operate with Algeria under colonial conditions? India does not have genuine co-operation in mind when she talks of collaboration. She uses the slogan as propaganda designed to mislead world opinion and deceive Pakistan.

Is the quarrel with India eternal? Eternal quarrels do not exist, but eternal interests do. Pakistan can maintain her vital interests only by confronting India until all disputes are equitably resolved. It is an article of faith of the people of Pakistan that the day will come when the people of Jammu and Kashmir will link their destinies with Pakistan and that Pakistan's other fundamental disputes with India, affecting the eastern parts of the country, would also find a just solution. The people of Pakistan want relations with India without entanglement. Confrontation which means neither peace nor war must be continued as a measure of self-defence until India realizes the need to settle all important disputes with Pakistan on the basis of recognized international merit and in a spirit of equality. India is not a Great Power. She has territorial and other disputes with Pakistan, and she seeks Pakistan's liquidation but not the encirclement of China unless it serves her own ends. Confrontation with India is, therefore, unavoidable and the only present answer to the solution of Indo-Pakistan disputes, the only way to achieve lasting peace between the two sub-continental powers. It is not a struggle between unequal powers as it would be in the case of confrontation with a Great or Global Power. Admittedly, there is a relative inequality, but not absolute inequality. Besides, this relative inequality is counterbalanced by the justice of Pakistan's cause, the spirit of her people, the collaboration of the people of Jammu and Kashmir who resent India's occupation of their land and seek to join Pakistan in a common brotherhood, and the overwhelming support she has received from other countries, including that of the People's Republic of China. The roots of confrontation between India and Pakistan go deep into our history and will have to continue until the cause of justice triumphs, no matter how heavy the odds. Peace, denied to the six hundred million people of the sub-continent for centuries, can return only when the disputes are resolved. Peace, so necessary to eradicate poverty, ignorance, and disease, cannot come by the surrender of legitimate rights, but through their attainment. A policy of confrontation is not a policy of militarism; indeed, it often has the effect of averting a physical conflict. The only known means by which a nation can avoid military conflict is by total preparedness, not only in a military context.

Asia being in the midst of a great revolution, local upheavals and changes are to be expected and the leaders of Asian countries must learn to live with revolution, knowing that there is no going back and that the *status quo* is not for purchase. If they are unable to ride the storm of revolution, they have no business to lead. It may be that only out of a clash of conflicting interests will a final synthesis be found in Asia and with it a tolerable peace. A long and arduous road has to be covered from confrontation to co-operation.

Small nations have always struggled against more powerful ones for their freedom. The whole history of mankind is a struggle of the oppressed against exploitation and domination. The contemporary history of Pakistan is nothing but an example of such a struggle. The struggle before Independence was against an alien racial domination; today it is for preserving independence. The wheel of change has come full circle, bringing us face to face with the same ancient menace. We are no more a subject people; we have the attributes of an independent nation and the will to remain free; though peace is our ideal, the defence of our rights continues to be the supreme objective of the people of Pakistan.